MW01481998

Nikki Gemmell is the bestselling author of thirteen novels, five works of non-fiction, and, as N.J. Gemmell, six children's books. Her work has received international critical acclaim and her books have been translated into twenty-two languages. She is also a columnist for the *Weekend Australian Magazine*. She was born in Wollongong, New South Wales.

Nikki Gemmell

After

FOURTH ESTATE
An Imprint of HarperCollins*Publishers*

Fourth Estate
an imprint of HarperCollins*Publishers*

First published in Australia in 2017
This edition published in 2019
by HarperCollins*Publishers* Australia Pty Limited
ABN 36 009 913 517
harpercollins.com.au

HarperCollins*Publishers*
Level 13, 201 Elizabeth Street, Sydney NSW 2000, Australia
Unit D1, 63 Apollo Drive, Rosedale, Auckland 0632, New Zealand
A 53, Sector 57, Noida, UP, India
1 London Bridge Street, London, SE1 9GF, United Kingdom
Bay Adelaide Centre, East Tower, 22 Adelaide Street West, 41st floor, Toronto,
    Ontario M5H 4E3, Canada
195 Broadway, New York NY 10007, USA

National Library of Australia Cataloguing-in-Publication data:

Gemmell, N.J., author.
  After / Nikki Gemmell.
  978 1 4607 5306 4 (paperback)
  978 1 4607 0769 2 (ebook)
  Gemmell, Elayn.
  Suicide victims – Biography.
  Suicide victims – Family relationships.
  Mothers and daughters – Biography.
  Bereavement – Psychological aspects.
  Children of suicide victims – Psychological aspects.
362.28092

Cover design by Darren Holt, HarperCollins Design Studio
Cover photograph by Sue Daniel
Author photograph by Kathy Luu
Typeset in Minion Pro Regular by Kirby Jones
Printed and bound in Australia by McPherson's Printing Group
The papers used by HarperCollins in the manufacture of this book are a natural,
recyclable product made from wood grown in sustainable plantation forests. The fibre
source and manufacturing processes meet recognised international environmental
standards, and carry certification.

Here we go mother on the shipless ocean.
Pity us, pity the ocean, here we go.
Anne Carson

1

Have you ever done what you dread to do, identify someone close to you in a morgue, on that thin steel table? I did. Just now. And I have to write this out, to piece together what has happened into some kind of coherence. And because writing is my ballast through life's toss.

Carry me in on a stretcher from this experience, carry me in.

*

Air from another world. In this concrete box of another world, an other-world, that is hushed and windowless. It is a morgue. It is too close to death. 'The mouth is always a shock,' T, the coronial assistant, is warning us.

Eh? What?

Bird-like, half our age, a face marinated in kindness, T is doing her best to prepare my brother Paul and myself before we step into the viewing room where a body awaits us. A body that the police need identified urgently on this sunny weekend of too much life everywhere else. 'No one's ever prepared for, er, how the lips *look*,' T adds.

Here, now, stopped of talk. My mouth a fistful of feathers. In this public service waiting room that is too public service for its task. Glarily new, foreign. Neither Paul nor myself have ever stepped inside such a place. Morgue. The very word a moan, a sullenness. And this building has seen too much life, in all its variety; has seen what it means to be deeply, vulnerably human, too much. You can feel it. The too many tears in this sparsely furnished room of strategically placed tissue boxes. That's a lot of weeping. These walls, the collectors of tears.

Paul and I are bound together within the fresh shock of this world. It feels like us against everything else. It is all too new. Every conversation feels mined. Full of barbing surprises we do not want to know about. So we prefer not speaking, if at all possible. Can't. Much. Stopped. T seems to understand.

*

But so much. To ask here. In this public place of too much death. Unpicking the knot of whatever has gone on. Head burning. Yet my brother and I are treading carefully where we do not want to tread at all. And amid the weight of the un-knowing there are formalities to be carried out, fast. Like this. Identification of Body. Which we have seen in

8

countless television police procedurals that are nothing like this. This pedestrian world, and our mouths, stopped.

A rupturing. As I wait for The Identification. So that matters can proceed. I feel like a child who has done something wrong. Called to the headmistress's office and not sure why. Something is peeling away. Within. It is monumental. It feels akin to great splinters of ice falling from an iceberg, it feels like a slipping into vulnerability I have never known. Huge walls of defence are crumbling here. I am forty-nine for God's sake. Have never been this. Have never felt this.

So. Right. Not as strong as I've assumed. Cannot contain the vulnerability flooding out yet no one knows it is there. A vulnerability I've managed to contain my entire life and now, and now, cannot. I am hurtling into the unknown.

*

I look across at Paul. Just as stricken as myself. Does he, like me, know too much yet not enough with all this? Everything is too complex, messy, muddy. A longing right now for simplicity, that great medicine of life. For the fatness of normality. The restful quiet; all those nibbling little challenges of an everyday life, which are no challenges at all I now know.

Brain, flooded. With too much. With this death too close and branded suspicious. Which means police involvement.

A likely autopsy. Endless questions beyond it. And I'm the person who walks through Customs at an Australian airport blushing over the box of chocolates I do not have in my suitcase but am thinking about. Here we go on the shipless ocean, here we go.

2

'The mouth is always a shock,' T has said.

Paul and I do not understand. Need help here. Need help actually in more ways than one. A sympathetic smile warms her eyes; T is the coronial assistant to have. Can she speak for us too, talk to the cops, hold our hands?

'It's slightly open,' T adds.

Open. Oh. Right. A smile back at her. A nod. Crazed. This can be dealt with. Am I unhinged here? Great cleavings of ice, splitting from their iceberg. Need something to hold, to steady myself. No. This can be done. Yes of course Paul and I can handle it. 'I've seen her mouth open before,' too breezy, guilty as sin but not. 'It's how she sleeps sometimes.'

T frowns. Perhaps I am coping too well, perhaps she can see right through me. 'No, this is different. It's the ... set ... of it.' Oh. The thought of whatever that means hovers in the air. Paul and I are the amateurs at death and doesn't T know it. This woman with her background in counselling who is so gentle before us both. With the nest of hands at her stomach, with the expectant and compassionate face. She is here on this sunny Saturday for the countless reeling families before us and after us, here for the sudden, unhinging Friday and weekend deaths, for the bodies that have to be identified because the police demand it so they can begin their investigations and move the corpses on swiftly in this city morgue not built to purpose, and packed.

*

Head, work. Shaking it as if shaking a listening into it. Everything has to be concentrated upon, everything said from now on has to be carefully thought out. Words, filtered. Watchfulness, full alert. And T is giving Paul and myself the feeling that this is the first time she has ever spoken about the stubbornness of a dead person's mouth; as if this is the first time she has ever forewarned visitors who want to be anywhere but here, who are lost and scrabbling and dissolving in front of her just like us. Clever that. And we are like two small animals in headlights stopped before her. Holding each other. All we have right now, as broken as each other in this place.

*

T tells us we can touch the body. 'Kiss it?' I blurt, not even sure I want to.

It? It? What's this it? T nods. She's seen everything, her face tells us that. We can stroke it, hug it, hold it or none of that. T tells us there will be a folded blanket under the head. Another drawn across the chest. She tells us the hands have been carefully placed across the blanket and the feet will be bare. As if by giving us as much detail as possible she can get us through this, can lessen the shock. No. She cannot.

*

Another family – a huddle of eight – emerges from the viewing room. Red eyed, clutching hands, leaning in on tender arms. Another family at the morgue on this infinitely lonely, infinitely wild Saturday, going through what we are going through. As Paul and myself reel in silence within the baldness of the waiting room, unanchored. The past feels already antique. For that was the mother time, with a mother in it.

A well-dressed woman crosses over to us. I steel myself as does Paul. Can feel his subtle retreat because small talk is beyond either of us right now, connection unwanted. As we sit, bereft, on the stained plastic seats of grimy utilitarianism that seem like an insult in this place.

'I'm sorry for keeping you waiting.' Oh. The woman is speaking. To us. Paul and I look up. We shake heads in quick denial. Find a smile. Connect. For we recognise the bewilderment in her face, the vulnerability in her eyes, the

13

leaking nostrils beyond her control that her hand flutters to contain with a tissue. Oh yes. The body ahead of ours was someone extremely close to this woman and the death is a felling shock just like our mother's is to us; she is still processing her new existence just as we are. Paul and I both blurt out empathy, 'Please, no.' 'It's fine, really.' 'Take all the time you need.' 'We understand.'

In that moment, two huddles of grieving family look at each other. Nod. Smile. Beyond words. Beyond talk. All of us recognising that every person in this room has entered a strange new existence glary with fragility, all of us united by tenderness and shock. And even though we will never come across these people again the connection feels deep because of how we've all seen each other on this effulgent Saturday of a world outside at full shout, except for us. This dingy waiting room is sanctified in that moment by a something faint, a flutter of connecting humanity. It is affirming and good and then they are gone.

*

T indicates that it is our turn for whatever is next. The people behind the scenes are powering through this body-viewing morning. Hey there's sun outside. Paul and I steady each other and walk across to the viewing room, vulnerability helmeting us both. And there she is. In a tiny space barely as long as a coffin, on the other side of

14

a curtain that runs the length of the room at table height. Our mother is very much on the other side. A police officer, Constable B, is quiet in the corner. She came to my house yesterday with her grim news, she is shadowing me on this journey, watching. This is the reality now. Being observed.

*

So. We were not prepared for the beautiful model's mouth slightly open, askew, the mouth that had already set itself awry through rigor mortis even then, so soon. Not prepared for the cold in the flesh, the refrigerated chill that had already penetrated the bones; the body that felt triumphantly cold through every firm inch of its flesh. Not prepared for clawed hands curled as if in agony at some final, sudden resistance we will never know of, or perhaps it was merely post mortem's creeping clutch drawing the skin tight. Not prepared for the slight smell of death, even in this building of officious signage and standard, plastic, waiting room seat; they couldn't scrub that, oh no. Not prepared for this to be Mum.

*

It is not sleep. My mother's wilfully youthful body is stiff and unworldly and gone, utterly gone. To an other-world or

15

no world at all. Her haunting hands in agony's clench. I am alone now. Paul is alone. And so is she.

Wanting to hold her. My mother, Elayn. Lift her. Press her into me as she would ram me close whenever I was ill, even as an adult. She'd hold me tight and soothe that she wished she could take the sickness from me, as if she wanted to leech it from my bones; she couldn't bear to see a child of hers suffering; needed their equilibrium and nothing else. It is the most vivid memory of her love – a mother's unbound love – and now it is lost. The enveloping of it. Gone.

As are the conversations. The personal history, family history. It was all to come, all, until of course it wasn't. I've lost the calm of the cushionings when we were both at our best, for nothing was more wanted in life: to be loved unconditionally by a parent, to be cherished for exactly who we are.

*

The sense of abandonment. Here. In this place. The obscenity of that. The shell of our mother, the skin on her face already sinking into the hollows of her skull. Giving her that distinct, distancing, mask of death. It is not Elayn but an eviscerating absence more skull than life. It is our mother. It is not. And as I weep over her – I love you, I love you so much – I think, for a trick of a moment, I catch her mouth move in its familiar acknowledgment, a movement of infinitely small

16

regret. At what she'd done. To herself. To us. I'm going mad here. Splintering. Will not be put right. Never, no, broken for the rest of my life. Because I know too much.

*

Stroking and stroking the softness of the silvery blonde hair, adult now to the child. Harangued by the guilt, at the words never said before to her. In her living, brittle, waiting life, with such conviction or force. I love you so much.

*

My mother's facial skin is radiantly smooth in death. We ask T if she is wearing makeup. If someone's put it on her or if she did herself, before death. The flesh has the sheen of a creamy foundation. I tell T that makeup would be a signifier of intent, a sign that Elayn had prepared for the final dramatic moment, which would be very her. The beautiful woman, always so careful of appearances, presenting to the world her best self. Every day, for a good hour or so, the symphony of her preparation in her tiny bathroom. The rows of cosmetics plucked from their glass shelves, like a Michelin chef at her kitchen.

T plucks out a tissue from yet another strategically placed box and lightly runs it across Elayn's cheek – no, no makeup. The radiance is her beauty, luminous even in death. Of course. Yet already her features are shrinking into the bone, becoming skull-like. Uncannily just as my grandmother had looked in her final days in a nursing home, as death crept over her and pushed life out. Already something else is stealing Elayn from us. I can feel the greed of it in the smell; the mouth's set.

*

A lonely death above all. 'Hold her hand, Nikki, hold her hand,' Paul beseeches for I'm closest to the fingers on the steel table. He's standing back near her feet. I do hold Elayn's hand. Clutch it tighter than it's ever been held in its life. Need her to feel this.

*

In these reeling hours, an uncurling of something fresh within. I am becoming someone else and need a rescuing from it. A bringing in from this new world.

Unhinged: To separate, to disconnect. Upset. Confused. Mentally unbalanced, deranged. A basket case. Unglued. Yes that is good, the best. That is it. As Alice said in her Wonderland, 'I can't explain myself … because I'm not myself.'

3

Who was she, this complicated woman now lying before her shattered son and daughter on this thin steel table on a Saturday morning of too much life everywhere else? Nothing has ever been as dramatic in our lives as our mother's leaving of it. Elayn is more trouble in death than in life, and we were never expecting that.

So I write, in an attempt to understand – now, too late – what shaped Elayn and specifically her final act that has aroused the suspicions of the police. I can do nothing else but question, query, probe right now. The mystery of my mother and her death is crowding out everything else. So. To write a woman into being. To write her back. Because I am wintering into bewilderment here.

*

Elayn, gone. And the ceramic lanterns that my children have made. In shardy slivers at my feet.

*

Lanterns carried across oceans from London to Sydney. Snugged in a tiny wooden crate constructed especially for them by a removalist with careful hands. As he held up several delicate cylinders to the light he made a promise that he would keep them safe, to trust him. And after six weeks of reeling and bracing in a steel shipping container the lanterns were returned to me in perfect condition in their bed of compacted straw.

And now. Nothing of the lanterns left, irretrievably, at my feet.

The wind did it. The lanterns didn't stand a chance, poor buggers. The furious wind that an Aboriginal elder once told me comes into a community after death and sweeps the spirit away; sweeps the world clean of them. A snappy snarl of a wind lifted my painting that is the length of a man clean from its two hooks and crashed it down upon my row of lanterns that had survived a rolling sea journey. Take that, and that, everything that is cherished. Everything that is keeping you calm and quiet.

*

Nineteen of them. Different heights and widths, none higher than a pencil. Their brittle white glows with a honeyed luminosity when a tea light is placed inside and lit.

For the great exhalation. A ritual of solace, most evenings. Whatever country, whatever city I am living in.

*

Lumen is the consecrated light that enters sanctuaries and lumen is what these ceramic chronicles of collective memory created. I would loosen, every night, within the benediction of the light. Now they are in pieces. As am I.

*

Each porcelain cylinder had been stamped with geographical details from a specific pocket of the English countryside, from when we lived there. A world child-height and most likely hidden from adults. So, the prickling of blackberry thorns from Malmesbury. The rolling of conkers from Tetbury. The soldier line of twigs cloaked in moss from Edinburgh. The defensive swirl of an ammonite thousands of years old from Lyme Regis echoed in the spiral of a shell from Mawgan Porth. Also, the prick of a banksia cone from Sydney's Tamarama. The triangulated tip of a eucalyptus seed from Wollongong. A gum leaf's arresting slenderness from Awaba. Relics from spiky Australian holidays of a toughening up, when we would open our faces to the sun and walk through long grass barefoot, unlocked by the light.

Embedded in ceramic is the natural history of my children growing up. The earth they've raced across, the trees they've climbed. The blackberries gobbled that have been lazing over forgotten dry-stone walls, rockpools hovered above in poky curiosity, pebbles picked through and pocketed and later transferred to secret boxes in far corners of small desks.

Earthy treasures that were stamped into damp rectangles of porcelain which were then rolled into cylinders. Fired with held breath, for some didn't survive this final reckoning. Our little coracles of balm would then be lined up in our living room in whatever country we were in, their golden light flickering in the close dark. Porcelain tubes representing everything held dear. Simplicity. The handmade. Care. Creativity. The natural world. Memory. Family. Love. Light.

*

Pieces on the floor. Lanterns cracked. A fistful of feathers in a mouth. A world stopped. How can I step back into the world again, how can I recover myself?

*

I write to gain control. To steady the ballast. It is not working here. Going in circles, head hurting too much.

Everywhere, in every corner of my world, a breaking, a splintering. Brain not working, cannot write, cannot think straight, yes, despairingly that.

*

Kintsugi: A Japanese philosophy of repair. Involving broken ceramic, porcelain or earthenware. A shogun, five hundred years ago, came to the conclusion that treasured vessels which had been chipped or smashed should not be discarded, actually. Excuse me, there is use in them yet. They should be given the gift of attention. Repaired with threads of gold paste cementing the shattered pieces like river lines on a map. So. Flaws must be declared. Cracks made a fearless feature. The result: a fresh beauty. On a human not God-like scale. Shunning the rigours of perfection and symmetry; the Apollonian virtues of obedience. It is the beauty of failure, and only some people see it. Yet the lanterns, irretrievable.

*

Chips and flecks and slivers of sharpness. Pieces of brokenness. That need a carrying in from the world. A monumental repairing. If it's possible. No, not.

*

River lines of gold, binding broken porcelain. Yet sometimes the breakage is too extensive. Sometimes crucial, tiny, connecting chips are infuriatingly lost. Gaps, gaps. Leakage. *Kintsugi* involves the construction of three-dimensional jigsaw puzzles that do not always work. Pieces most wilfully do not cleave. Edges do not bind. Not everything is snug and in its place; the result is not always watertight. Sometimes the *Kintsugi* practitioner has to give up because the fragments stubbornly will not come together. It shouldn't be considered failure, that.

But everything feels like failure now.

4

T gently guides me, as if I'm porcelain, to an official form waiting in readiness.

Constable B, who'd been in the viewing room, is discreetly behind me still, following, watching. Yes, this was indeed my mother. Yes, I confirm all this. With the signature's flourish there is an ending of something. Officialdom's release. Into the next phase. T informs us she will call on Monday to discuss the coroner's decision about an autopsy. Paul and I tell her we'd prefer nothing invasive. T indicates we may not have a choice. That if we want to refuse permission – she hesitates – then we have the right to take it higher. To the Supreme Court? A pause. Yes, the Supreme Court. Oh. Everything a question, everything unknown.

T puts her arm around my brittleness as she walks us to the door. She says, softer, that she will also be ringing to see how I am. Wanting to weep at her kindness, cracked by it, not sure I can hold myself upright for much longer. I can call her any time. She hands me her business card.

'Does Mum really have to be cut open?'

Hesitation. Treading carefully now. A licking of the lips. T says the doctor and coroner will most likely order an autopsy. There's too much uncertainty over the death. So, autopsies are only sought if there's a medical mystery with the deceased and in this case, er, yes, there is. The police's hovery presence is telling us this. Autopsies are expensive and will only be undertaken if something of benefit arises from them. Like certainty. And don't we all need certainty with this one.

So. A pathologist will most likely want to dissect our mother's beautiful body. A microscopic inspection of her internal organs will be carried out and a biochemical testing of her stomach contents. It will be brutal. No, no dignity here. And an appeal from us will only hold things up. 'Delay, you know, the body.' For the funeral. Paul and I both throw up our hands and say, 'Whatever'; whatever the world of officialdom thinks best. They need to investigate as do we. Paul and I also have our suspicions. The inquiries will not necessarily be intertwined. We don't tell them that.

*

A last question as we leave, to Constable B. I feel I know something of her now, that in return for her watchfulness she might, possibly, give me a small gift: honesty.

'Was it deliberate?'

26

Constable B nods uncertainly. She can't speak. Her eyes say she's sorry, that she wishes she didn't have to tell us this.

*

And the lanterns. Broken at my feet. From the furious wind. A tsunami of too much.

*

Walking outside into the blare of sunshine and the roar of a weekend diving into life. We blink like theatre goers who've been immersed in a drama of darkness for a gruelling afternoon yet it's only been an hour. Exhaustion like a rake is dragging through our bodies. Our walking. Can't, at a normal pace. Can't see properly, think. I am not inhabiting myself correctly. A normal self is somewhere else.

'Do you want me to drive?' Paul asks.

'No, I can do it.' Rubbing my head as if it'll rub clearness into it, like an alcoholic after a big night out who needs to find their way home from an unknown gutter.

*

Weaving through traffic. Not sure how. So much to process, organise, do. 'A funeral?' Paul asks. Elayn's wishes? A blank. Slipped into the earth where she's spent the past forty years of her life or returned to the place she grew up? That she never visits. Nestled close to her parents or closer to her grandchildren? Buried or burnt? Scattered to the wind or kept in a vase on a shelf? We never asked. Any of it. Too hard, awkward, soon. The weight of uncertainty, about getting everything right, on top of all the disquiet about everything else.

Elayn was so particular about appearances and her funeral would be no different. Particular about getting things just so, right. Paul and I are heading into a storm of more questions the closer we get to home. More phone calls, interrogations, judgment, as news spreads within her circle and we try to explain what we can about what we barely know ourselves.

Floundering here in the unhinged dark. Can't drive properly, a danger to others and myself.

*

As is attributed to Gautama Buddha, 'In the end, this matters most: How well did you love? How fully did you live? How deeply did you let go?'

How well did I love? Not well enough.

5

Was my mother ever sure of her daughter's unconditional love for her? No, there was always too much complexity for the clearness of that. I'd remarked to girlfriends that when Elayn died there'd be a sense of relief mixed in with everything else. A catch of guilt as I said it, but it was the truth and the truth, spoken, always felt soldering and right. I told my girlfriends I'd be freed, finally, like a diver bulleting from the depths of pressured darkness into light. How wrong I was, how wrong. I did not expect my life to be hell without my mother in it. I know, even now on this day of morgue, that this will be the case. She's got me well and good.

*

Margaret Thatcher said in an interview that she had nothing to say to her mother after the age of fifteen. So cruelly true, for so many females. The girls with wilfulness blazing under their skin, impatient for their own lives and paths;

wanting, needing to break away and contemptuous of their mothers' choices. Daughters too quickly dismissive and judgmental, with their mysterious, self-absorbed velocity. Daughters who think of their mothers as the happiness stalkers, reining them in with tut and affront. Daughters so caught up in their own fresh worlds. Their mothers can only cling to the edges and the girls can resent even that.

The clutter of maternal attention. The fury at attempts to persuade, nudge, shape. And then, and then, sometimes between them, the descent into the piracy of silence. From either side, from both sides. Which was Elayn and me. Oh yes, we knew that old friend – The Great Withholding – that crashed between us at times. And toppled us both.

*

Yet there was so much love over the years, without us even realising it. Without acknowledging it, nurturing it, or asking for it. And in Elayn's final year the dynamic between us of frustration and fury, hauteur and head butt softened, miraculously, into something else. Everything opened out like a stop-motion film of a shy flower finding light. We were both tired from decades of adult wariness and clash and let go, stepped back, let each other in. Who knew we could evolve to this? Yet we did. And it astounded us both. Like two old warriors who'd had enough. Who'd softened into a knowing, finally, after years of exhausting attack.

31

Softened into a realisation that none of it, actually, was worth it.

*

'If I had my life over I never would have had kids,' Elayn threw at me once. It was a phrase I carried throughout my adult life, particularly when I had children myself. Yet when Elayn and I were close, at our best, those resonant lines from the Psalms dropped over me like a benediction: 'The darkness is no darkness with thee.' Close, it felt like I was suddenly bathed in a vernissage, a varnishing, and all the sullen textures of my daughterly being were combusting into light. I craved that. Never stopped being that little girl aching for a demonstrative love, to be dandled on a proverbial knee, trying to nudge my way in.

*

Elayn spoke of death with yearning yet vivacity coursed so strongly under her skin. All contradiction and inconsistency. As Dorothy Parker said of Isadora Duncan: 'There was never a place for her in the ranks of the terrible, slow army of the cautious. She ran ahead, where there were no paths.' In the 1970s we had lift-off: she finally dared to be herself. Changed the spelling of her name – pedestrian Elaine to audacious Elayn – following a flirt with numerology. She embraced divorce when no one around her, in sleepy suburbanland, dared do it. Stepped into the world of topless bathing. Biorhythms. Male centrefolds in *Cleo*. Transcendental meditation and star signs. All were glorious liberations from the swamping of model-wifeliness she had been trapped in for decades. She did everything too well. T.S. Eliot said that most people are only a very little alive, and during that time Elayn felt like one of the few – the fortunate, spirit-brimmed few – who are the over-livers.

In the seventies, in her late thirties, Elayn found the courage to be magnificently, courageously detached from the world around her. It was the time of her Great Acceleration.

Yet she had come of age two decades earlier, an era when women were not expected to work. Married at nineteen, a mother at twenty-four, her husband's property. Elayn belonged to the last generation of females to exist in that world. She chafed against it. Grew to loathe it. She straddled three eras. A pre-feminist one as she remained buried in suburbia for two decades of marriage and motherhood; a feminist one of liberation and exhilaration involving, principally, the younger women around her; and then the post-feminist era that was her daughter's. It was Elayn's tragedy and bitterness to have been born when she was. She was too modern for her surroundings for much of her life. Possibly, also, in her death. There will be many future Elayns.

*

The Great Acceleration. The breaking free. The brokenness. An ungluing that either does you in or doesn't. Sometimes, with *Kintsugi*, the vessel refuses the calling of shape. Abandonment is sometimes appropriate, alongside an acceptance of loss. It's the texture of life.

*

Elayn had a young girl in her who refused to die. It was in her curiosity, her ready smile, her red lips. She was an appreciator. She never under-lived. That's who she was in public. But she was someone else in private. Gabriel García Márquez said that everyone has three lives – a public life, a private one and a secret one. Can we ever really chisel out someone's secret life? The ugliness of the underbelly, in all its rawness. Exposed most viciously with those closest to us. Those, of course, that we love the most.

*

What will survive of us is love and we must hold on to it, only that. To enable those left behind to move on, to repair. Must hold on to love and not the wasted times of argy-bargy and grump, not the assault of shutting off and the cruelty of indifference. Why did Elayn and I hold ourselves hostage to that ridiculously negative energy of affront at various periods in our lives? It achieved nothing. What a waste.

6

So. We'll never smell Elayn's smell again, the brew of soap and Vitamin E cream and White Linen perfume and powder. A smell we'd known since childhood. As an adult I lived in London for almost fifteen years and at the end of a stay Mum asked if she could change the sheets for me. 'No, leave them,' I'd murmured, but didn't say why. Never told her that that night I'd snuggled up in the bed she'd used, still stamped with her smell, and deeply slept. Because for that one night I'd craved the security of childhood, the time long ago when my husband, Andrew, and myself didn't live like this, far removed from what shaped us, from our land, our sky, our heart.

*

On Elayn's birthday, one English April, I bought a tree. A eucalyptus. Fifty pounds – Christ! – from Portobello Road. A sapling of silvery coltishness with rounded, juvenile leaves. It was startling with difference. Bought to celebrate the earth opening up to receive its springtime benediction, the air cracking open. Bought to plunge us home. Scent us back. The Australian native took to the sodden London soil and grew tall. Its rounded leaves sharpened into familiar slivers. Their colour, a faded blue-green; a striking contrast to the rich English greens all around them. Just as Elayn was always a striking contrast to the world around her.

Occasionally, throughout the yearning years, a gum leaf would be plucked and crushed and held under my nose, just like I used to as a child. Breathed in deep. Brimming with memories of home. Of living under the great thumb of nature and your skin drinking in the light like the desert with rain. And brimming with the memory of Mum. The good times. The essential, repairing times that were craved, always craved. Because when we were good I felt better.

*

Elayn loved the row of porcelain lanterns. It was intended that the children would make some for her, too. We never got around to it; they were always too beautiful and we kept them for ourselves. Our tight little family of six, our tight little world, and Elayn on the edge of it. So much guilt. The elderly, pushed to the edge of our lives. In the great rush of our lives.

*

I had two grandmothers, Lexi and Win. Both lived to one hundred and the family fully expected Elayn to do this also; our women were strong. My mother had several decades of living left in her; her vivacity the outward sign of it. She never allowed herself to be rubbed out, erased. By men, by other women, by life. Until this. Whatever this is.

*

As I go through Elayn's address book and break the news over and over – but not the nub of it – I become painfully conscious there are so many gaps in her back story. It was all to come, all; we had plenty of time for the telling until of course we didn't. And as I mine Elayn's address book for clues I marvel at the secrets of her existence. This slim volume, like a tiny vault, guarding a hidden life.

An address book that is a map of being. If only it could be deciphered. To reconstruct Elayn with repairing threads of gold. An address book alive with secrets. It contains the numbers for six different lawyers, a famous television personality, a hotline for the Victims of Child Abuse. *What?* Elayn's parents are dead as are her two brothers, which means much of a past life lost. A watching dog inside me, patiently waiting for answers. I cannot bear the corrosiveness of uncertainty, have never been able to deal with it.

Elayn had always existed vividly in the present. I was never curious enough about her past. What child is? Do we ever really know our parents – as women, as men – rather than as mothers and fathers? The richness of their other lives, beyond us. Perhaps we don't want to know them too well for the truth would be too painful to bear; that they had unknown existences, desires, impulses; that we were not, perhaps, at the centre of their world. Actually.

*

Un-maternal mothers do exist. They should not be judged. And they, like all mothers, treat various children differently within the family dynamic. Which is why this is my story and not Paul's, nor my oldest brother, Mark's, who was not with us during the first fortnight of Elayn's death. Elayn presented herself differently to all of us. I cannot speak for my siblings. They knew a different Elayn, as did all her friends. Their Elayn is not mine nor mine theirs. I barbed her, by my mere existence. I have always struggled to understand why. Few of her friends would know this.

Kafka said he wrote to close his eyes. But you can also write to open them.

*

Sometimes, within a pit of fury, Elayn spat out to my younger, vulnerable self what felt like the arrowed truth: 'Everyone hates you.' 'You're so ugly.' 'You have no friends.' Yep, she knew the Achilles heel. My vulnerability as a child was no deterrent for her. She knew how to reduce like no other, as mothers do. But this betrays the complexity of the woman. Of course I recall the flung words yet Elayn was so much more than that; as we are all so much more than our worst selves. But that particular side of her was what was recorded in my journals in the heat of the hurting, from the age of fifteen onwards. It's before me now in furious, tear-stained scribblings.

The writer's chip of ice. Even then, as a teenager. Elayn knew it and was afraid of it. For the family as much as herself.

*

Samuel Johnson wrote that his life was one long escape from himself. My life was one long escape from my mother, from the woman she wanted as a daughter. In adulthood I lived in a lot of places far away that were resolutely not 'home'. Nowhere near the flinch of that. Until the end. The final five years of Elayn's life when I returned after decades of gypsy wandering. To deal with my past. Or not.

Unglued, yes. Perhaps that was her intention. Take that, and that. And my life feels as if it has been in rehearsal for now. This motherless, anchorless time.

*

Paul and I are freshly adulted and we do not want this. It hurts, for both of us, to be in this place. Everything is upended, it all feels too late. This narrowing family, this unquiet air, as our little family shrinks to its huddled few.

And in the thick of it, the yearning, home-sore. Needing to get back to my little teapot of a house and its enveloping warmth. Wanting to stay bunkered for a while, for what feels like months, years, in some necessary ritual of mourning, sheltered from the tug and the pull of the world. Wanting to get back to before. Hiding from the future. From police questions. From the ramming curiosity of the neighbourhood. From my four children most of all. What happened, who is to blame? If anyone, if all of us. 'How did Nonna die, Mum?'

Serenity's guard is gone.

7

A modern story for modern times.

Elayn Gemmell euthanised herself. I have difficulty saying the words: 'committed suicide'. Because that bald and emotionally fraught word – *suicide* – is not often thrown around among all the talk of dying with dignity, which implies rationality, forethought, calm. Yet *euthanised* doesn't feel right either. It has, too much, the whiff of the science lab to it, the face mask and nurse-administered needle. *Suicide* implies the unhinged and irrational, the fatally weakened; *euthanasia*, the clinical assistance of someone else. Euthanasia is neither spontaneous nor sudden. The perpetrator has agency.

Neither word feels rigidly correct.

*

Paul and I, suddenly at the coalface of this Dying with Dignity world. We didn't choose to be. We don't know much about it. Here we go mother on the shipless ocean, here we go.

*

Fact: Elayn Gemmell euthanised herself, by herself, in an armchair in front of a blaring television. Just as summer was blazing into the year. Just as her family were straightening their backs after winter's clench and holding their faces to a soaring sky. Yet all of us were unaware of how deeply, fatally despairing this woman in our midst felt during this lovely, lighten-ing time. All of us were unaware of the tightness of the noose around her life.

*

I was the last of Elayn's three children to see her, four days before her death. One of her sons had not seen her for several weeks, one for months. What exactly to call what happened here, with Elayn's vanishing from her children's lives?

Slipped away. Decided. Actioned. Slept into death. Assisted with suicide. Voluntarily assisted dying. Dying with dignity.

Elayn went underground. She did it her way, as she had done with so many things in her life. This death, above all, was so very her.

43

*

The builders found Elayn. They had been taking their time renovating her bathroom. Had left her without it for weeks. Telling her they had another job to go to then another and they'd be back soon, no worries; again and again. They'd left an elderly woman without a bathroom, shower or bath. A proud and beautiful female – always exquisitely dressed – was making do with just the laundry sink and a tiny spare toilet. She was sponging herself among the washing powders and fabric softeners between visiting my house to shower every few days.

The exhaustion of it. The shredding of her dignity. The annoyance at having to carry a showering kit whenever she visited. Elayn had entered a new world of invisibility, of the little old lady whose wants could be brushed off. She had specialised throughout her life in image control but now, for the first time, she could not. The builders could never give her an end date to their renovations, they kept springing on her a fresh flit. The stress of uncertainty, and she hated it as much as myself. In some respects we were so alike.

*

'If I knew what this renovation entailed I never would have started it,' Elayn sighed the last night I saw her. She was stranded in fret. But she didn't complain much because that was the way of her generation. Stoic, accepting, recognising the pressures of modern life; while others, younger, complained more. So the builders went to those more voluble clients. The squeaky wheel gets the most attention, we all know that. Elayn was the little old lady who was easy to brush off, who wouldn't give them too much grief. Until she did.

*

A Friday morning. Elayn didn't answer the door. The foreman and his men let themselves in with their spare key. The bathroom was a shell of freshly concreted walls. Boxes of heavy tiles were stacked on the carpet outside it. And there was Elayn. With a bottle of Baileys Irish Cream and an empty pill jar beside her. At first the builders assumed she was sleeping.

The Baileys, ah the Baileys. A nod to seventies cocktail loucheness because Mum didn't drink except for the occasional celebratory glass. A final indulgence; plunging her back to an era where she felt smart and sophisticated and empowered and in control, her world on fire. The years of her Great Acceleration. Those soft-focused Baileys ads from long ago would slide into our suburban world with their golden promise of other, better places and smoother lives.

*

Elayn's television was still on, the tableau carefully planned. Who would see it, who would not. So very her. She was like a horse kicking out strong with this final scenario. Her last, protesting, gesture. Fuck you, builders, fuck you. So, just a little old lady, huh? To be shunted to the side of your work, put off, given the flick, abandoned. Right.

*

Elayn had been in chronic pain. She had had a foot operation eleven months earlier to eradicate a heel spur among other things. She'd been plagued by foot problems in her later years and blamed a gruelling regime of ballet practice as a child and years of unsuitable footwear as an adult. Stilettos, wedges, corks, clogs, platforms, pumps, you name it, her shoe choice had charted the history of fashion at its most audacious. She revelled in the lift – physically and emotionally – they gave her. Until she could wear them no longer, for they had crippled her. In her later years Elayn was retreating into a shell of pain. In her final weeks she was curved like a comma around a walking stick. Agony was hardening around her. Changing her. Consuming her.

*

My mother had booked herself in for the foot operation at one of Australia's most prestigious hospitals. If only I could travel back in time, before the surgery, and talk to Elayn, ask her, 'Why are you doing this? Are you sure it's the best option? Is this really necessary at your age?' There's anger, now, at a medical system that allows elderly people to undergo such surgery – at enormous personal cost. Physically, mentally, financially.

*

When I visited Elayn in hospital, after her operation, the foot looked wrong. The toe next to the big one had been shortened. How was that meant to work? Surely it would affect her entire gait? For an older woman, was a dramatic toe-shortening really necessary? There was a pin with a plastic pearl ball on its end, stuck through the length of the appendage. Elayn was excited about how pretty it looked; her glamorous new adornment. I now know she was off her face with new painkillers that had entered her life; giggly with happiness, energised. She took a photo of the pretty pin. Posted it proudly on Facebook. 'My foot with jewel on the toe!'

*

Everything about my mother's foot looked painful. Out of whack. But what did I know? I was as ignorant as my mother. She was happy; I was happy. I didn't talk to the surgeon and should have. He was nowhere to be seen post-op.

'He was so arrogant,' Elayn told me, months later, when I begged her to go back for corrective surgery. 'I couldn't bear to have anything to do with him again.' Her call. The way of her generation. Accepting, stoic. The medical profession perhaps relies on it; that aversion to making a fuss. Perhaps we all do to some extent.

*

Elayn wrote me an email describing her pain:

> I'm in a desperate situation because every step I take
> is like scissors digging into my groin, back and right
> leg, causing excruciating pain and making me almost
> immobile.

*

The surgery had broken her. A fortnight before her death she'd been weeping over the phone to me, sobbing with the abandon of a child, telling me that she dreaded going into care and losing control of her life, dreaded becoming a burden. It had left Elayn with a spine thrown out of kilter, twisted around a walking stick like a withered crone from a fairy tale. And Elayn had never been that, never, truly 'old,' nor impaired. My mother was utterly, emotionally, naked. Stripped to her bare self by pain. Her voice was conveying that there was no way out, no clear path from this mess. I had never witnessed such vulnerability in her. The sobbing like a little girl, the fear. The mother had become the child. I wish the surgeon had known of it. How he had reduced her. I was furious. And helpless.

'It'll be okay,' I tried to soothe, believing that there must be some upward trajectory out of this pain, into the light, Mum just had to wait. I was ignorant back then of what pain does; that it sometimes cannot be managed. Because with chronic pain there is often no sure path to recovery, no map away from it. And pain's diminishing is often only a temporary fix. I didn't bother to find out any of this when my mother was alive. Elayn knew. In hindsight, I was shamefully naïve.

*

The surgery left my mother with a pretty pin good enough for Facebook plus an opioid addiction. She had a flirtation with painkillers – specifically the drug OxyContin – immediately after the operation, which rapidly became a reliance which developed into something else. After several months the drugs began to lose their potency and then the overwhelming, debilitating pain nestled back into my mother's world as her constant companion who she could never shake off. And so like a junkie desperate for her next fix, my upstanding, product-of-the-1950s mother launched herself into the murky world of doctor shopping. She was seeing GP after GP for this and that and on top of it having cortisone injections and scans every other week to find the source of the pain now piercing her body in several points: foot, thigh, hip, lower back.

She was hoarding pills. In hindsight, that felt far too easy; that she could do this. But she had been broken by the foot operation. Was facing a future of uncertainty, dependence and fear. During a scan the week before her death my mother was advised that she really shouldn't be using her car anymore, the pain in her right leg was too deadening and debilitating. Elayn had to face the fact that her driving days were over. That zippy black car languishing unused in its garage was the final blow. Driving had always been a gift of independence.

*

The pain was also sapping Elayn's looks. For the first time in her life she was going unnoticed, morphing into just another little old lady people brushed past in the harried whirl of life. My mother had never been invisible. The realisation was sapping her strength. In her final months she tried to break free from the wily, triumphant pain holding her strength hostage, but she could not. There was no 'fix'. She could no longer present a beautiful face to the world. The sheer exhausting effort to quell the agony was brittling and breaking her. Her signature lipstick was not often worn in her final weeks. A bleak truth: medical intervention harmed my mother and eventually tunnelled her into death.

*

Euthanasia, from the Greek, means Good Death.

Was it?

In Ancient Greece suicide didn't have the stigma it does now. It wasn't considered an action of the depressed or mentally ill. Athenian magistrates kept a supply of poison for anyone feeling the need to kill themselves. It was a matter-of-fact response to debilitating illness or pain or incapacity. Official permission was all that was needed. Hemlock was preferred, usually in liquid form. The creeping of the cold, as the limbs become leaden. The awareness, the horror, the inability to turn back. Is that a good death?

*

God-botherers changed everything. They declared that suicide was not a rational choice but an attack on the hegemony of their God, an unforgiveable insult to Him.

The only will that should decide a person's death was God's. Those who took their own life were to be punished particularly severely, in hell, the shame so great that their families would also be penalised. Monetarily, and by social disgrace. Remnants of that attitude linger. I can feel the whispers even now, greedy at the door. The shame, the shame of it. The familial failing.

*

Elayn spoke occasionally about her Dying with Dignity forums and importing euthanasia drugs from Mexico; the necessity of choice; celebrities who support empowering death decisions and the importance of Do Not Resuscitate directives. She carried a business card spelling out a DNR wish in her wallet. I didn't listen enough. To any of it. She made it all sound cultish, faddish. I would get emotional, cry, 'But don't you want to see your grandchildren growing up?' I would cover my ears like a child, shake my head. Because it felt impossible that such an accomplished seizer of life could want anything but life. And so I condemned my mother to an infinitely desolate, infinitely lonely death.

*

My mother had an abhorrence of many things: not being given a choice to end her life exactly how she wanted to; loss of voice; the thought of a nursing home, which would mean an inability to access pills which would give her agency over her death. And this the woman who had championed independence, and control, her entire adult life.

Elayn was a proud woman who couldn't choose the quality of her life, but she could choose the quality of her death. Ahead, as she saw it, was a bleak certainty, involving several decades of semi-life in a Home of the Forgotten, Removed and Left Behind. As an elderly woman told me afterwards, scratch most women in their seventies and you'll find a fear of that world, and a desire to kill yourself at a time that you choose if your quality of life deteriorates that much. To have control over your own fate.

All, so very, Elayn.

8

My mother's despair seeped into my life; it was the harrower of my peace. This at a time when I was struggling to keep everything on an even keel: four children aged four to fifteen, plus work, plus husband, plus household. It was a fraught time of failing at everything; of nothing having my full attention; of boxes-to-be-ticked completed in harried snatches and then every night around 3 a.m. I'd be harangued awake from a fitful sleep with the swamping of it all, too much in the head, too much. At 3 a.m., bang. Big eye. A term used by Australian Antarctic expeditioners, explaining the time when you cannot sleep because of the endless, blinding, hurting light. Big eye, yes, that was it. Harassed awake every night by the endless, blinding light of anxiety, churn, distress.

Elayn's pain felt ragingly unfair. So triumphantly immune to intervention. How could that be in our rampantly medicated modern lives? Exhaustion was consuming us both. I was finding it difficult to drive, thrive, complete tasks; cook at 6 p.m. then help with homework and bath time;

bugger it, the kids could go dirty, have cereal for dinner some nights. I was falling asleep at two o'clock before the school pickup because I had to, couldn't train my body out of it, and because my nights were tormented by big eye too much.

*

The woman's lot. My generation's lot. Both ends, yep. Looking after the kids as well as the parents, holding down the job, sorting out the husband and house and feeling like you're not doing anything adequately. Drowning in busyness. And after every summer holiday as the kids are heading back to school there's the sickening feeling that this new year is starting on the back foot once again, that you'll never quite catch up. That ahead are endless mornings of an alarm shrilling you awake, which is the signal to jump on the mouse wheel all over again. Your life is your children's. As is the money earnt and holidays and visits to the bathroom, secret stashes of chocolate and good night's sleeps. A moment for a sugar fix is furtively snatched as is the tweezering of hairs from the upper lip. You don't actually have your own life, or privacy; your existence is spent in service to everyone else. The sanctity of a secret life no longer exists.

And all around me, a world in thrall to the Temple of Speed as I'm screaming inside to retrieve something for myself. 'You never stop,' my father, Bob, said in horror

55

once, from the perspective of a different, slower life. I know we have to develop defence mechanisms. The ability to pause, recognise the gifts of stillness, recalibrate. But they feel like essential life skills I don't have. Elayn was aware of the madness of my working-mum life. She'd escaped that world herself. When I, her youngest child, turned eighteen she stopped cooking. She'd had enough. Of the thankless giving, as a mother, the sheer exhausting depletion of it.

*

An email, a week before Elayn died:

Darling Nikki and Andrew,
Firstly a big apology for imposing on your busy lives. Any help you can give is very appreciated and will only be until I can finalise my situation. EVERYTHING is so.o.o slow. I am needing to get a carer and finding it all very hard. I am too scared to drive as my right leg feels dead. I don't feel safe driving. Only if either of you, or anyone you know who I can pay, can drop me off in Bronte Road for a shower and acupuncture today it would be great. So sorry my darlings, I never envisaged I would be in this situation, but then 'why not me!?'
Hugs Nonna xxx

*

A month before Elayn died I rang Bob, who lives six hours' drive away. I begged him to ring my two brothers to ask them to somehow share the load of our mother's care; it was too much on my own. I didn't hear from either brother.

In Elayn's final weeks I tried again. Asked my mother if I could organise a family get-together to discuss her future care. 'Later, not now. I'm too tired.' As if it was all too much.

*

Elayn's story begins in a small mining town called Meekatharra. In the Western Australian desert. The era, post-Depression.

After her dusty baby years with a mesh-covered cot and a lawn of dirt, her family moved several thousand kilometres across the wide brown continent to the Hunter Valley of New South Wales. Elayn's father was a mining engineer, an agitator in the Engine Drivers' Association, a communist. Her mother was a Barnardos kid sent to Australia from a London care home aged eleven, and trained for service despite a keen intelligence. Service was expected of girls like that, nothing else. It left my grandmother with a lifetime of bafflement and hurt about how she had been railroaded as a child; sent from institution to institution. A hedge of masculine will surrounded her. As it did Elayn. It shaped their lives. It didn't stop them though from kicking out strong, both of them, in revolt. Again and again. No one was going to impose control on them. They wanted that for themselves.

*

Elayn's childhood world: a deeply masculine landscape of rodeos and country pubs, bushfire alerts and floods. A place pockmarked by coalmines and coated in black dust but a place where nature nonetheless pressed close. Yet my mother wanted a bigger world than the small mining towns of the Hunter Valley, hamlets of sullen tranquillity. She wanted to suck the marrow out of life. Men who were different. People who lived by the book rather than the earth. And a country town of narrowed eyes and neighbourly sourness wasn't for Elayn; the energy between the community and her felt wrong. She left school at sixteen because that's what girls from towns like that did. They weren't meant for education, nor the la-di-dah world of the Big Smoke. Neither were the men. They were expected to go down the pit from their mid-teens. As my grandfather did at fourteen, and my father at sixteen. Only the truly exceptional got out.

*

But then there was her beauty. It was Elayn's calling card into another life. In her late teens she was crowned Miss

Hunter Valley and swiftly noticed beyond her tiny world. She became a model. Was sent off to the longed-for Big Smoke. Photographed by some of Australia's most iconic photographers, Max Dupain and Laurence Le Guay, for some of the nation's biggest companies. Her modelling diary records the jobs in a beautiful, adolescent hand. Rothmans, Remington, Frigidaire, and the department stores David Jones and Hordern Bros. Elayn had a fierce determination to shake off whatever was holding her back. To get Somewhere Else.

Yet a young coalminer from the same high school was after the Cessnock 'looker'. He won. And Elaine disappeared because that was what was expected of girls from that world. And because her husband, my father, demanded it. Bob never knew much of his wife's modelling life. After she died I showed him the iconic ads she'd been in. It was the first time he'd seen them. Elayn was adept at secret lives, hidden pockets, that people close to her were forbidden access to. A pattern in life, and in death.

The beautiful coalminer's wife stopped modelling. Had kids. The family moved to Wollongong, four hours south of the Hunter Valley, to begin a new life on new coalfields. Bob bought his wife the Great Australian Dream, a house with a verandah. Then a bigger one. In the suburbs. Which closed over her. For decades.

*

But Elayn didn't want to be the supporting player in someone else's life. A restlessness propelled her. Her mind was hungry, sharp. She grew out of wanting shag-pile carpet in the lounge room and a cabana by the swimming pool. When I began school Elayn started exploring the world of work; not something that suburban housewives of the seventies necessarily did. Pre-children, she'd been a hotel receptionist. She landed a job at the national telecommunications company of the time, Telecom, in Wollongong. Lift off. Elayn suddenly had her own money again. Glamour and independence. It was an exhilarating unfurling. After twenty years of marriage Bob and Elayn divorced. I was ten. Mum and I moved to the Big Smoke, Sydney; the court ordered the boys stay with their father. Elayn had finally found her 'great good place' in life. Henry James coined the term – it means a special place of calm and retreat that's just for you, no one else, a place where your eye rests. Where upon arrival you exhale. The prospect of it: a renovation of your serenity.

*

So, to the Great Affirming. The Great Acceleration. She set about turning herself into who she really wanted to be – the woman she'd kept under wraps for so long. The pronunciation of words like piano became pi-arn-o in a rigorous scrubbing of the past. Elayn wanted to be seen as sophisticated, to fit in to the big city life. Thought her new words made her sound cultured. To me, they did the opposite. To me, Elayn never completely shook off the coalmining dust that shaped her early years. She hated me for thinking that; hated the fact I was proud of my coalmining origins when she wanted to bury them. So the dance began.

*

Elayn was determined her daughter would transcend the claustrophobic world of her childhood. Have the opportunities she never had. She took me to ballet matinees, plays, gallery openings, music recitals. She followed every diet fad of the era: our kitchen cupboards were full of spirulina and slippery elm and the most stolid of mueslis; at one stage, for years, we weren't eating eggs because of the scare campaign over cholesterol. She sent me to elocution lessons. Pushed me to sit for a scholarship for Kincoppal, a prestigious Catholic girls' school. She needed to blot out the stain of our former world. The pit, the uncouth voices, meat-and-three-veg dinners, the inarticulate, clogged men. The white bread and chips as opposed to pasta. The World Book Encyclopedia as opposed to the Encyclopaedia Britannica. The tabloid newspapers as opposed to broadsheets. And commercial TV stations as opposed to the ABC, for the national broadcaster was full of voices that didn't sound like Wollongong. Like us. Both of us acquired new voices in our new lives. There was the endless push into talking proper – 'nothing, not nothink, Nicole,' 'just not jist,' 'yes not yeah,' 'you not youse,' 'something not somethink.'

*

I remember the mortification that on my scholarship application, Elayn used as a referee a Wollongong gentleman who ran a bottle shop. 'How could you?' My wail of embarrassment, aged eleven.

But Mum knew no one of standing, no doctor or lawyer as a friend. She explained that, 'You have to be responsible, to hold a position like that.' I won the scholarship, the path to my transformation set. By Elayn. By her determination to spare me the world of her own youth. And because I didn't have the looks that had rescued her. 'Can you just *try* and make yourself a little less ugly?' she'd cry in despair when I first put on reading glasses in my teens.

*

Elayn had not been to university, had not completed high school. She was appalled that after school I chose to do Arts after getting the marks to do Medicine. Mortified when I swapped from the University of Sydney to the Institute of Technology to complete my degree. As brittle as an old bone at my graduation, uncomfortable and angry. Years later she'd whisper to those close, 'She doesn't even have a university degree,' failing to note that the institute had become a university while I was still at it. It was just part of the great embarrassment of how I'd squandered my life. How I never got into television. Never did the prestigious degree. Never made her truly proud within the narrow parameters she had set for herself. At least, that's what she conveyed to me. She left me hanging for my own good. To toughen me up no doubt. I never did.

*

Elayn fought her entire adult life for a voice. A say in her own circumstances. She instructed me continually on the necessity of independence: not to rely on a man financially, not to end up with a controlling male. She was often turtled by bitterness over her past, it was a carapace over her life she could not completely shake. Women who are free spirits often lose the one thing that's special about them when they marry, and Elayn was determined to never make that same mistake twice. Post-divorce, various boyfriends asked her to get married but she always declined, explaining to me, 'Men. They're so boring. All they do is talk about themselves. And want sex.' Increasingly, as Elayn aged, she turned to her female friends for joy.

*

Finally, in her late thirties, my mother became the architect of her own life. The magnificence of the transformation. With her divorce settlement she bought a flat in Sydney's trendy Eastern Suburbs and a sports car. Carved out a living for herself in the corporate sector as an office manager for Telecom's videoconferencing centre. Worked in a skyscraper in Australia's most dynamic city. She'd come a long way, all by herself. Had finally found her place in the world. Was steeped in belonging, for the first time in her life.

Elayn's narrative from childhood to old age was characterised by audacious disruption. Erasures of a younger, more pliant self. Her existence was never quietly clearing its throat but banging on the table, roaring to be heard. It was a life of reinvention and transformation, of moving on and breaking free, and it ended as she was sailing into insignificance, in a flat in Sydney, with great determination and grit and enormous, bloody-minded loneliness. And I will never recover from it.

*

Death was Elayn's last magnificent act of breaking free. Right until the end she did it her way. Yet her final act left me 'exposed on a high ledge in full light', as Virginia Woolf wrote. But so be it. Because in the Grand Ballroom of Destiny Reversal, beautiful, vivacious, enigmatic Elayn Gemmell reigned supreme.

ELAYN'S MODELLING DAYS

Latest model

THIS pretty sun-worshipper likes a radio to keep her happy at the beach. She looks pleased with a new transistor portable, of a type now on the Australian market.

9

Elayn was careful. She had done her research. When police officers came to the house and informed me that my mother had died they also pulled out a pad and took notes. Now I know why. Her children could have been the subject of a police investigation if we'd had anything to do with the circumstances; we could have been facing a charge of accessory after the fact. I did not know this at the time. Police officers, their faces clamped by solemnity, had never been to my house. But I knew what their presence signified.

*

'Nicole?'

Instantly, the chest is clutched in a cliché of dread. Something is calamitously wrong. Instantly, an internal buckling. These faces can only mean one thing. 'The children?'

'No.' The officers are quick with reassurance. They have done this before. But their faces are not letting me off. 'Can we come inside?' The young female officer doesn't want spectacle, at this too-public front gate.

'My husband?' A quick shaking of heads, no, thank God no, as the three of us are enveloped by the house's embrace. 'It's your mother.' As soon as the door is shut. I know in that instant that Elayn is dead. How she's done it. And why.

*

The world shifts in an instant. I become an adult, in an instant. My mother as a woman – an autonomous, thinking woman – reveals herself to me, just like that. Yet I keen to the heavens in shock; she did it, actually did it. Without telling any of us. And if I'd written of her slipping from this earth in a novel in these circumstances no one would believe it, yet here it is, the police, in front of me, with their hard truth.

I need a wall, a floor, something solid to prop me up. I am reeling. Slumping on the bottom step of the stairs in the kitchen, leaning against the wall, held by it, needing the earth and its grounding. The police officers crouching beside me. 'We will not leave you, Nicole.'

In that moment my entire perception of a police officer and what they stand for has veered. Whoever puts police officer, and tenderness, in the same sentence? I do now. Well, well.

*

The body's discovery, a few hours beforehand. A crime scene because that is what you do with situations like this, situations of oddity and the unknown within a home. My mother was in front of the telly. *The Bachelorette* finale had aired the previous night and I hope she had got a good old giggle out of it. Yet I do not ask the police what channel was on, it feels like an intrusion too far. The officers went through my mother's flat. They questioned the builders who had called them. The men were told to pack their tools and leave. The police took items from Elayn's apartment. Evidence. Oh.

*

I ask the two young officers if I can make them a cup of tea; they both decline. They are working. Of course. We're all studiously careful and gentle. They ask if they can ring someone for me. I'm incapable of ringing my husband myself. I stumble out Andrew's phone number. The male officer, Constable R, goes into the lounge room and rings him, man to man, and reports back that Andrew will come home immediately. It will take about an hour for him to extricate himself from work. 'We won't leave you,' Constable B, the police woman, repeats.

These young officers of lowered voice and careful tone stay by me the entire ocean of time of lurching and motherless alone, as I weep, and wail, and recall and try to work out; as I run to the bathroom and blow my nose on toilet paper because the tissues have all been used up; and as I try to raise various relatives but none of them are picking up – too many answering machines, too many messages left. Where is everyone on this sunny Friday lunchtime; at the café, the pub, revelling in normal pre-weekend life; the zoom of it, too much, everywhere else.

*

Can't make it. To a chair. To sit on. Constable B stays on the floor with me, refusing a chair herself, a drink, a vegemite sandwich. I have to say something, am babbling, talking too fast amid a sloppy dissolving. 'Our priority is you,' they keep saying, the drum beat through the conversation. Because of what Mum has done, perhaps, because of a fear of a copycat response. So. Right. I am that broken in front of them that they fear for me. 'This must be so hard for you, to always have to do this,' I say.

'Our priority is you.'

*

In the thick of it all, yowling loneliness. Grand Canyon vast. At this new way of being, already. How long will it last? Till the end of my days, perhaps, the end of days.

*

69

Trying to recall, explain. An older woman's desire to be noticed. Heard. Taken seriously. When all around her was a world brushing her off. Prioritising other people and other jobs. That rendered her invisible. The builders, the bloody builders. Myself.

Darling Nikki and Andrew,
Firstly, a big apology for imposing on your busy lives …

The guilt. I know I am trying to explain too much.

*

Several months earlier, Elayn had told me she would give me warning about any euthanasia situation; she would never spring it upon me. She had said this with a fervour that made me believe her and trust her and there was solace in that. I had felt that if she was ever reaching some kind of endgame with all this, she'd let me know. Prepare me however she could.

Now, disbelief. And an ice-cold drenching of knowing. Of course she did it. This is Elayn.

For ten years she had been saying on and off that she wanted to kill herself, at the time of her choosing; that she was a great supporter of the euthanasia movement. The offhand comments had been triggered by invasive surgery to eradicate thyroid cancer a decade ago. She suspected

70

almost a lifetime of dyeing her hair had caused it – Elayn had started going grey at nineteen. After her thyroid was removed a thin scar ran along her neck as if her throat had been slashed. She told me she never wanted to go through such a procedure again; that next time, she'd 'just go'. Without medical intervention.

For several years prior to her thyroid operation Elayn's blood cancer levels had been raised but doctors couldn't find where a tumour was; for several gruelling years my mother had submitted to all kinds of proddings and probings to find the sickness locked within her. Finally the thyroid was pinpointed. She had learnt her lesson from an ordeal that dragged out over several years of endless waiting in endless specialists' surgeries. For Elayn, in her final decade, quality of life was everything. And empowerment, and control, and choice.

*

'Was it an accident?' I stumble to the two police officers. Needing it to be so. Some terrible slippage from the administering of pain relief, a muddle of pills; would we ever know for sure? Constable B says an empty bottle of pills was found next to Elayn. Oxycodone, otherwise known as OxyContin. I've never heard of either of those. I stammer out my ignorance. Constable R takes out his notepad and asks more detailed questions as I explain through tears what I know and do not. Look at him closely. The intent way he's writing. The situation is shifting into something else here. 'Has Mum done something wrong?'

'We just need to work out what's happened.'

Have *I* done something wrong? The dawning. That this being here for me might, actually, also be something else. An investigation.

*

Brain, racing. What have the police been told? Has something illegal happened here? Have I implicated myself? Mum? Talk, suddenly, rationed. No idea what I could have done wrong – or Mum. Just an overwhelming need to suddenly protect both of us. There'll be no mention of drugs from Mexico; she had talked about importing an enabling drug like Nembutal and no one in the family quite believed it. Yet, yet. The police have seized Elayn's copy of *The Peaceful Pill Handbook*, the bible of the Australian euthanasia movement. I didn't know she had it. Of course she did.

*

The constables reassure repeatedly that Elayn looked peaceful, that her passing would have been serene. They explain that as well as the *Handbook* they have my mother's keys and handbag. I have no idea what else they were looking for, what they took. Except for my mother's body. Yes, the ambulance took that.

*

Neither constable has heard of Dr Philip Nitschke, the contentious doctor at the forefront of Australia's euthanasia movement and author of *The Peaceful Pill Handbook*. Their lives, despite being police officers, seem innocent of old people and their wearisome concerns: of dying with dignity and empowerment, a dread of nursing homes and the cruelty of chronic pain.

Constable B seems so youthful, so un-hardened by life; she could be my daughter. Her brow is furrowed with concern as my nose runs freely and my eyes weep with rawness. I hope my own daughter grows up to be someone like this. So decent, empathetic, and at such a young age. 'This must be hard for you too,' I repeat, motherly, barely knowing what I'm saying anymore.

'It's my job.'

Constable R is more pragmatic. He has a job to do. He needs to know Elayn's movements the previous week.

*

Right. Elayn had asked me to drive her to an Automatic Teller Machine. It was the Sunday night before she died.

She was going out to dinner with us. When I picked her up from her flat the first thing she wanted to do was get cash, $2000. I was shocked. The amount was so much. We would be paying for her dinner, and no one in my world carries that much around in their handbag. 'What's it for, Mum?'

'Things. Life.'

'The builders?'

'No, I pay them by direct debit. I just need it.' Elayn was irritated. Didn't want to talk about it. Clutched her purse tighter as she sat in the passenger seat. I let it lie. Annoyed she wasn't being straight with me; thinking 'funny, batty old woman', well and truly a member of that odd and ancient species now; addled by distrust and keeping her money in the proverbial shoebox under the bed.

But where did all the cash go? The police want to know. They didn't find any in her flat. The scribbling in Constable R's notebook intensifies.

*

As the police officers ask their questions, a world stopped; bleached, glary white. Ahead, endless explaining, talking, and I've never felt so far from the truth.

*

74

I shouldn't have let the cash question lie. But like so much else I did. Treading carefully. Needing a soothing in the relationship, too old now for anything else. One of the reasons I'd returned from London for good was to be with Elayn and I didn't want a homecoming marred by the furies that had blighted our adult relationship for so long. We were both exhausted by the situation. Had become used to letting things lie in those last years; to not slipping into the default position. We were both too tired now for the roar of offence and attack and outrage, which happened too much in the depleting old days.

*

Elayn knew she came a distant sixth in my world after the children and husband; I never carved out a pedestal that made her feel special enough. 'Can you pick up my salmon from the fish shop, Nik? It's ready.'

'Mum, I'm at soccer trials. Nowhere near it. An hour's drive away.'

'No matter. I'll work it out.'

In the final weeks phone calls like that were increasing. There were sudden summonses and orders out of the blue and they were impossible to always carry out with the rest of the family clogging up the hours. I begged Mum to give us notice, to slot in requests at least a day in advance so the cram of the days could be managed. I didn't have a clean path to Elayn, to all her needs and wants. It was always a juggle, eating into time I needed for something else.

*

I let Elayn down more than once. Was often somewhere else. My life was so regimented by the demands of four children that I couldn't abandon everything at the drop of a hat. There were always sporting fixtures and playdates – some several suburbs away – work meetings and children's parties and the salmon remained uncollected more than once. Or Andrew would go to pick it up and the order wouldn't be there, we'd have no idea why. Was the pain disintegrating Elayn's mind? She would ask me to make a doctor's appointment that I was to drive her to, then would cancel at the last minute; or she'd ask me to cancel for her. Everything was becoming tricky, unreliable, pesky. But I did it. When I could. Which was most times. The rare times when I couldn't blare loud in my memory.

*

This was the woman who drove hours to get me to country eisteddfods as a child, sometimes in dresses she had copied from *Young Talent Time* on the television. The bottom line: as an adult, I wasn't there for my mother enough. Should have dropped other things more. Never gave back to the extent that I should. But does any child? Elizabeth Jolley said that the child can be concerned for their parent but their energy can't be spent going backwards; the child's is a forward-going tie, not mired in the past. Do adult children sometimes use that as an excuse? We the children, so distracted by other worlds.

*

The police officers are told that in her final weeks Elayn was doubled over in pain. That she was heavily medicating in the final days of her life. The police officers are told of her buoyancy in our final conversation, on the Tuesday. Constable B explains that suicides are often like that when they've made their choice. Elayn seemed energised, motivated. It is often the suicide's final, joyous, lightness of being. They are released.

*

Going in circles, back tracking, head hurts. Five days before Elayn killed herself, the Sunday. We had made an agreement that night to check in regularly with each other because I was worried; it was a new ritual of care between us. Late that evening Elayn sent some beautiful photos of my eldest son, known as Ticky, from her phone. Monday, no word. Tuesday, worry. I rang. She said she was taking a lot of pills, and sleeping a lot. She sounded buoyant, as if the great weight of pain had lifted. The builders were on a break. 'I can't talk Nik, I've got so much to do while they're not here.' Elayn was firing again. Finally, I felt, there could be light at the end of the tunnel. Wednesday, no word. But I didn't worry, because I felt we could finally be on that upward trajectory. I sent an email checking in on the Thursday. At 5 p.m., a reply.

Nikki I'm ok. Just bombed out on drugs xxx

I assumed this meant Elayn's regulation painkillers. This was her last email to me. No indication of intentions, no illuminating final message, three kisses but no last words of love or motherly acknowledgment. The haunting of that. Did she love me? Did she care?

*

Thanks for telling me mama. Really reassuring to know.
Love you x

I don't know if Mum ever got my email in reply. It was sent shortly after 5 p.m. The police tell me it's unclear if she died on the Thursday evening or Friday's early hours. As I search up these final emails the police are swiftly behind my shoulder. Noting down time of sending. What exactly had been said. Tone, no doubt. Of all of this mess.

*

Everything takes on a different meaning now. The Baileys by her side. 'But Mum doesn't drink!' Nothing makes sense. It all feels irrational, and despairing, and too sudden; a fit of pique. Drinking? 'Well, only on social occasions. Like the glass of Prosecco and orange juice, just like me. At the last dinner. It was enough for both of us.' The memory of her zippy happiness as we raised our glasses for the birthday toast. Or was that just mine?

Constable B: 'She ordered in alcohol from a home delivery service the day she died. The builders told us. They were there when it came.'

Oh. Secret pockets in secret lives.

*

While the two constables watch, I can't get on to any of my immediate family. No one is answering. Minutes tick away. Bob has been divorced from Mum for forty years, bitterly, but our family is still entwined; he had seen Elayn at my house a few weeks previously, when she dropped in for a shower while he was staying with us. But I need a parent. Right now. Need the reassurance of knowing I'm not completely an adult, yet, that there's someone still out there for me. I'm such a jumble here: desperately adult and child at the same time.

Finally I track down my half-sister in Armidale, six hours away by car. Dad isn't with her. I stumble out that Mum has died; that I need Dad. She understands. He's a short drive away. Within ten minutes he rings. In his response I catch the vestige of a love not seen for forty years, a rhythm of partnership. The one image of tranquillity I have of them is of the folding of the bed sheets in a dance of coming together, the strange, slow waltz of it, perfectly in sync. These two people had made three children, and parented them, and it was all in Dad's voice now, bereft.

I couldn't raise Paul, who lived in Newcastle, several hours north. Dad would get one of my half-brothers to drive to him, they live close to my brother. Within a fractured family of steps and halves we are pulling together. 'Do you want me to come down? I'll drive right away.' I smile. My love for him fierce. Tell him no, it's too far. This is something I have to deal with myself; he went from my mum's world almost four decades previously and it doesn't feel right to reel him back into it, now.

*

Andrew arrives. He envelops me, in shock. But the fact he is here, strong beside me, is a step into repair; into facing the world. The police leave. Paul rings. 'Oh Mum, oh Mum, oh Mum.' I've never heard my brother weep. He is as I am right now, I can hear it in his voice. The disbelief, the desolation. That she actually did it, that we didn't listen enough.

*

The telling of the story. Again and again. Shock, disbelief, from all of us. Crying, 'No, no,' at the phone. 'What? What?' Elayn was too vibrant, too alive, for the sordidness of this. Yet I was the only one of the family who saw her in those final weeks. When I saw her curved in pain around her walking stick, and fighting it.

*

Paul drives several hours to join us that Friday night after an afternoon of pacing in his flat. 'Was it an accident?' we keep asking. We need the solace of that possibility, because the other is too momentous to think about. 'The police think not,' I say. No, no comfort, for either of us. That'll be a long way off. Both of us feeling peeled here, skinned; for everything about our family has been laid bare, in all its inadequacy. As a family we haven't been good enough.

*

No farewell note. No clue. No explanation. A suicide note would have allayed police fears, negated the 'suspicious' tag. But no, we're not to be given the dubious consolation of that. A medical officer has certified death but not signed a death notice – which means it is suspected the death was not natural. So, welcome to a world of suspicion. Doubt. Rationing answers to official questions. Red tape.

*

In the fraught world of euthanasia, I say this: if the perpetrator's family cannot, by law, be involved in the wishes of the person wanting to die, then you're condemning that person to a horrendously bleak and lonely death. And there will be many people left reeling in the wake of that death. People who have to find the body. Hear the news from police that their relative has died. Identify the body in a morgue. Submit to a gruelling police investigation. Deal with unanswerable questions. And find it difficult to extract themselves from the situation, to firm themselves from the mess of it.

*

Paul and I, broken in one corner, and our older brother, Mark, in another, holed up in Newcastle during all the demanding official business of death then far away in China on a business trip; his choice. Paul and I did not understand the absence of Elayn's first born during this time, the mystery was a burden to us. Yet as Jane Austen said, 'Nobody, who has not been in the interior of a family, can say what the difficulties of any individual of that family may be.' To me, during that time, it felt like the Gemmell family had suddenly become a liability, a great weight to now carry through life. I'd never turned a forensic eye on my family. More than anyone else, family members had always been great mysteries to me. And none more so than its matriarch, in life, and in death.

*

Some days are seared in a very white light on your consciousness, and remain that way; their hurting light will always be with you. That Friday when the police came is one of them. Was this all about Elayn? Or was it that she didn't want it to be about her any longer? The burden of her. To all of us. We could have done it, could have gotten her through. Yet Elayn wouldn't let us.

That day of the telling was the last day of my old life, my young life, when I had a mother in it. A mother with a secret life and she would never let me in; who'd organised a lock and key for her bedroom during the time I lived with her. Right to the end she was ring-fenced. Prior to the arrival of the police on my doorstep now feels like my 'Before' world, which seems a very long time ago. From the moment the officers said, 'It's your mother,' I have existed in another world, an After world, which is less carefree; brittle, unbalanced. My state, now, is Demolished.

10

To the children.

In the fragile hours after the police have gone on their way and before the kids arrive home from school, Andrew and I agree that we will not tell our little family too much detail of Elayn's death. Cannot bring ourselves, at that point, to articulate what we barely understand ourselves. 'Nonna died in her sleep.' We will leave it at that. Yet dancing around the truth only curdles the situation. But I did not know that then.

*

The news is broken to Ticky, the eldest son, as he's picked up from the bus stop. He absorbs the loss of his beloved grandmother like one of those buildings folding in on itself in a controlled moment of destruction. Right. Someone else to worry about amid the wreckage of all this.

*

'I want to walk,' the teenager clotted with emotion says, shrugging his mother's arm away. He climbs out of the stationary car and strides off with a furious, lone velocity. 'I need to be alone.' I'm struck by the chasm that sometimes opens up between mother and child – deep, uncrossing; motherhood at its most helpless. At a time when I just want to cleave him to me. Smell his vulnerable softness just as I used to when he was a child; stroke him into a soothing. The knot of him now feels somehow like blame.

*

All the grandchildren called Elayn, Nonna. It was her commanding choice. Nanny or Granny or Gran? All, she felt, were too aging. My very modern choice, G? Too obscure. Yet she loved the European warmth of a nonna. Loved her grandchildren effusively in a way she rarely did with me. Ticky and her talked often; she had spoken of her pain to him. He had helped her many times with carrying groceries or shifting boxes around in her flat; he had helped her shuffle up the stairs to her flat, or down the stairs to our front door, always a careful arm over her shoulder.

*

An hour or so after Ticky's recoil from the car, Andrew goes searching the neighbourhood for his son. Finds him sitting against a wall on the beach, by himself. They sit there, in silence, man to man. Andrew rings to alert me; I leave them be. Another world. Fierce and fragile with love for them both.

The gratitude, deep in my core, for my husband. Amid all this. That he's here, continually solid, enfolding us, laughing us up. 'Your caring for me as you do almost overwhelms me. It is so real, and so strange,' Virginia Woolf wrote of her Leonard and yes, oh yes, my Andrew too. Later on this vibrating night of too much he catches my eye across the chatter and we smile our grim secrets. My love for him glows calm like a candle and at no time more so than now. Yet I never tell him of the thankfulness for this deep, rescuing love. Should. Must.

*

Thirteen-year-old Boh weeps and wails with a head thrown back and mouth wide; the Greek chorus loud enough for all of us, keening anguish to his heavens. He sobs like a toddler abandoned at a shopping centre. And at night asks if he can snuggle up beside me in bed. Needs to. Presses close. All of us anchorless here, all of us needing some solid thing to hold on to.

*

The eight year old, nicknamed Biahbi, is frowning. Calm and thinking and perplexed. 'But Nonna is still in her flat,' she insists. 'In her chair. She's not dead. We can't speak to her but we can see her.' What is my daughter understanding here, or not? What is she going through? She's as impenetrable, and fascinating, as her grandmother. Elayn loved taking her only granddaughter to shows; dance performances, the circus, musicals. The last one they saw together was *Matilda*, several months previously. A girly treat, with sushi beforehand and chocolate at interval. I'm not worried about Biahbi on this fragile night. She's my strongest of the lot.

*

And then Jages. Just four years old, he's the afterthought. Never meant to be on this earth. When I skipped a couple of periods in my mid-forties I thought it was the menopause galloping too soon into my life. He was our astonishing mistake, nudging into the tight family unit when we assumed our little posse was complete. He has tipped Andrew and me over the edge with exhaustion, but he fills out our lives with a soldering delight; he makes us all laugh so much. Within our family he exists solely to be loved; there are no expectations upon him, no pressure nor stress; he is the kissing post we all gravitate to, often, when we need enveloping. Like now. His response to the news of his grandmother: 'So sad, so sad. Poor Nonna.' As if he is understanding, and accepting, most of all.

*

What bleakly adult world have the older children been plunged into with all this? With their Nonna's choice to leave them, without a word. All the family is coming together in fragility and shock, everyone is processing their grief in wildly varying ways. There is the calm of Biahbi, Andrew and Jages on one side but then there is the rangy rest of us. In pieces, like the ceramic lanterns.

*

Andrew puts out little spot fires of howl, makes dinner, runs baths, scoops up lone children from the beach and laughs them into silliness with stinky bum jokes. As if he's trying to pull us away from these selves we are becoming, these new selves. I remember the night of our wedding, almost two decades ago, the man I married trying to make me laugh; the great distractor who does it magnificently. May he never grow up. Over the years I've wanted to wipe the floor with him at times and he's wanted to do the same with me (more often, I know, than I have with him). He's seen me at my ugly worst as I have with him. (Why is it easiest to hurt most the people we love? Perhaps because we know, all too well, their Achilles heel.) But it's as if the ingredients of mateship, affection, admiration, duty and respect have combined over decades into a rich brew of deep, quiet love. I now know there are two types of love: unanchored, consuming, romantic love, where all you want is the other person; and the great calm of true love, where all that is wanted is the other person's good. And so it is with him.

*

Andrew knew Elayn well. The woman behind the mother. Her complexity. He had seen her trickiness over the decades and sometimes did not agree with it but was ever the diplomat; careful, retreating, but often silent with anger at how she treated us. To her he was the man with the beautiful, broadcaster's voice, who wore a suit well and a lovely tie impeccably, the son-in-law she always wanted to have.

She had made it known, vocally, how unsuitable all of the previous boyfriends had been. Not only to me, but to them. 'Your mother doesn't like me, does she?' said N, long ago, a man I was going to marry in my twenties. The sadness, to hear him declare it so baldly, because of course it was the case. It became a stain between N and me that neither of us could scrub off, that my mother didn't like him and never would. Another notch in the tally of daughterly fury.

Yet in hindsight Elayn was right. N was a serial flitter, and perhaps she perceived the weakness in him right from the start.

*

The last time we all saw Elayn was at Ticky's fifteenth birthday, four days before her death. We had taken her to a local Greek restaurant. We knew the owners well. They had made a fuss of the family matriarch as she hobbled in on her walking stick with her brave, warm smile. It was an occasion brimmed with laughter. Elayn had taken the photos that she would send me later that night, of her grandson almost six feet tall. She had laughed, 'You're as handsome as a movie star.' They had discussed her latest-model smartphone. It's how they often bonded, Ticky the enabler of Elayn's electronic life. Perhaps that night cemented her enormous decision, as we hooted and joshed as a family around the merry table: Andrew and I and the kids were happy, wewould be all right, we would carry on.

*

Ticky's birthday will be scarred from now on as the memory trigger for the final time we saw Elayn. Every year, as another birthday clocks over for him, we as a family will remember the death of my mother too. Can I forgive her for that? For that beautiful boy, now broken at the news that his life-brimmed enthusiast is gone. Elayn gave him unjudging love, as grandparents do. And as much as I love my children, unstintingly and constantly, it sometimes feels like I can never give them enough – that there's a great open wound with each of them at times that I'm pouring my love into. What is going on in there?

I sensed, often with Elayn, that there was some great wound there too. But she wouldn't let me in. My need for some kind of spoken love from her never let up. I was forever the little girl wanting to be loved, butting my heart fruitlessly against a brick wall. Now, I hold my children close. Tell them I love them, constantly; get 'love you' back.

Our little family. This is love. This is everything. All I have now. I've parented differently to Elayn. Existed within a marriage differently. Have watched and learnt and spent decades acting in opposition. No, daughters do not necessarily become their mothers.

*

Boh cries out in his sleep in whimpery pain. I press closer, jam my body to his; want him to know the solace of maternal warmth even as he slumbers. Coiled anger, wolfish, at what my mother has done on this day. To all of us. So many people to look after here, in the aftermath; so many mysteries to work out. All around us, a wide, uncertain sheet of ice, cracking and bowing, that cannot support our weight. Did Elayn think of the consequences of her actions for all those around her, the children as well as the adults? Children more than adults. Her mother, Win, used to say Elayn had a lack of empathy for some of us. Her theory: that her daughter was always the centre of attention as the stunningly beautiful child; that the world revolved around her, always had; so many of her family enabled it.

Elayn barely saw Win in her final years.

11

I'm not good at being alive right now. I'm not sure I can be pieced together in any way that resembles a former self. My brain is not working properly, it feels like I've had an axe blow through the head that will never completely heal. What is needed, a holiday from uncertainty. Instead, there is brittleness. Snappiness. With everything. As I walk the days, pick up kids, shop for groceries, drive. Nervy, jumpy, a collision in my head of too much. I cannot do gatherings, crowds, am abandoning commitments, forgetting to return emails and calls; forgetting a friend's gallery opening, a birthday lunch. I've lost my writing confidence, it no longer sings; sentences won't come; the brain will not grind into gear. The well of words is depleted, I am bankrupt. In a typical instant I can't find the name of the type of cheese you put on pasta or a synonym for the word 'reduced'; it is as if a massive short-circuiting is spitting and fizzing across every aspect of my life. Editors, readers, a wider world knowing nothing. All around me are writers losing their jobs or being asked to work for a pittance or nothing; this is no time to be trashing a column gig. Yet it is so hard to go on; to work through the weekly slog of fresh thought when there is none. I can't talk confidently at newspaper functions like I used to, can't find buoyancy. I'm angering old friends who don't seem to understand the depth of the blow, but how could they? Prickly and shelled, hollowed and felled.

*

I should have been at the coalface of the situation, right beside Elayn. And not just ringing and emailing but banging on her door. But I wasn't. Too busy, distracted, the child always listening to the parent and accepting meekly what they said; the child not questioning and not grown up enough. I couldn't bear to hear Elayn's wish to die early, at the time of her choosing. It seemed too easy and defeatist and selfish. I wanted the formal certainties of the old ways of death and life; everything in its time and place. But Mum wanted a different certainty.

Pain was overruling everything. Veering her destiny. Robbing us of her. Winning.

*

Constable B couldn't spell my suggested cause of death as I was hunched on the bottom kitchen step, rammed into the wall. 'Euth – in – asia?' she asked.

'It's euth – *an* – asia.' I carefully sounded the letters out. 'And I'm only just getting my head around that myself.'

As the questions bulleted into me, ping, ping, ping. 'How long had your mother been planning this?' 'Do you have any idea of her mind frame?' 'Did she talk to you about pills?' 'Did you help her with anything that would have enabled her to do this?'

All these questions fired at me, and darting among them, all the questions I had of myself:

'Why did Mum drop this on us?' 'Why no indication of her utter despair towards the end?' 'Why didn't she leave us a note, if only to say she loved us?' 'Did she have any idea of the emotional depth charges her actions would detonate within so many lives?' 'Why didn't she let us in?'

*

Catapulted into crisis. As surely as a hysterectomy launches the menopause. Ticky, Boh and I watch the film *Still Alice*, needing a distraction from all of this. An academic specialising in language falls under the bus of early onset dementia. 'That's you, Mum,' my sons joke. I can't laugh. There's a creeping sense of panic, a tide coming in. Ahead, a drowning. And it will be a silent one; like a submarine sinking beneath the surface. As I hold myself together for everyone else.

*

Perhaps in the end Elayn thought it easier to just go it alone without the shambles of familial complication. To take matters into her own hands without the emotional clutter of all of us.

*

'What was it exactly: empowerment, or despair?' I posed the question in my weekly column. A woman who had tried to commit suicide by overdosing with pills wrote in answer:

> Nikki, the reason people commit suicide is simply
> the suffering is so great you cannot bear it another
> minute. It's as simple as that. You don't think about
> the devastating effect it's going to have on your loved
> ones because of the level of suffering you are in. It's not
> empowerment, it's despair. You don't think of how it will
> hurt your family – perhaps for life – because your level
> of suffering is so great you cannot bear to live another
> minute.

Perhaps, perhaps, that is closest to the truth.

*

British comedian Caroline Aherne, commenting on her suicide attempt when she mixed three bottles of champagne with antidepressants: 'I actually have no recollection of it. Finding out what I'd done was like finding out I'd stabbed fifteen people. I would never knowingly hurt people in that way.'

*

With her final act Elayn has altered my future. She had been attempting to do this since my teenage years, to mould me into something I didn't want to be. It was easy for so long to shake her intentions off; I was wilful, stubborn, strong; knew who I wanted to be and was able to veer along my own, very particular, path. But finally, with this, she's got me. She has crushed me.

Wanting, now, to shed people, complexity, the cram of chatter and especially questions, so many questions about what happened. I don't want to talk, to explain, can't soothe others in their grief because I need soothing myself. My nights are harangued by too much in my head and I've never known sleeplessness like this. Then days, the poking and prying of chinwag. As Virginia Woolf wrote, 'On the outskirts of every agony sits some observant fellow who points.'

'How did Elayn die?' 'What did the coroner say?' 'When can we find out?' 'Why are police involved?' 'You must ring me when you have news. I *must* know.'

Carry me in on a stretcher from this experience, carry me in. I've no strength for it. For *them.* The village gossips, present and past, poking and plucking, cawing and crowing, from various pockets of Elayn's life and all out now in fulsome force. No strength for the gossipy beaky pry of them, for their endless phone calls asking if I'm okay but then slipping into the nub of what they really, actually, want. 'What really happened? I *need* to know.' And not only them but friends, neighbours, colleagues, everyone; overwhelmingly, everyone.

*

Flinched. That my mother killed herself. That it reflects too much on me, on our failures as a family. I do not want spectacle, accusation, judgment. 'Elayn died in her sleep. We're waiting on the results of the autopsy. Then we'll have a clearer picture.' Too easy to say, and technically true. But I'm shying away from flinty honesty. Only my closest mates know the damning details; they're the only ones I have the courage for.

*

Right now, all I want is to be enveloped by our house's shielding embrace. But the doorbell rings again and again, people drop in spontaneously, there are flower deliveries, scented candles, books, emails, texts. Meals, so many meals, mainly spaghetti bolognese; one friend from school places rose petals on the plastic lid. The bounteousness of community; the reason why we returned from London after all the years of exile, and it is good, so good, affirming. We are strong in this world and this world is strong around us. But I am drowning in the midst of it. No one knows. Not even Andrew. I am holding it together. For all of us. Huddled against the world.

*

On the final Sunday evening of Elayn, I had driven her to our house for a shower after dinner. On the way through the rabbit warren of local streets we had paused again and again as neighbours were greeted, out on footpaths and verandahs for the sunset and their dogs. Elayn, in the passenger seat, commented, 'You have such a community around you, Nik. It's good.' Did that drive, like the joyous dinner, enable her final act in some small, accumulative way? Enable her to leave us, thinking this, that we're strong, we'd be all right? But I'm not. I'm not, Mummy, I'm not.

*

Still the flowers come and the candles and the meals that no longer fit in our fridge. A week later, two. I feel guilty, teary, swamped; don't want to explain, talk, but it's the expected transaction here. It's all too much. It's all lovely and caring and affirming but we're weighted down by blooms, the house looks like a funeral parlour, it's crushing in on us, all the jugs and buckets have been requisitioned as vases as well as every surface. A longing for clean, clear space. The known again. That lovely swell of normality when your world feels plumed and I'm not sure that it can ever be back.

*

Secrets and lies. No, I do not want my children to know there's a suicide in the family, particularly the older ones, the teenagers. Will it rub off on them? Unhinge some deep-seated and destructive vulnerability? My eldest sons are on the cusp of adulthood. They were tinderboxes of bravado and vulnerability, tenderness and strop even before Elayn's death – volcanically hormonal combinations of anguish and explosion under immense academic pressure at a selective school. Elayn killed herself a week before their big end of year exams. And we live by a sheer sandstone cliff towering over crashing surf. One Christmas Eve four men dangled their legs off the edge and jumped. A pact. One survived.

'Nonna died in her sleep.'

I need to cave our little family, protect all of us from the onslaught of exhaustion, weeping, whispers; want to cave myself. The Victorians had the right idea, retreating and mourning their loved ones for six months or a year or several; as does Judaism, with its one-year period of mourning that is only, specifically, for the loss of a parent, because it believes it's a particularly striking absence which requires a longer period of adjustment than for anyone else. A clear stretch of time, specifically for immersing yourself in gratitude for all that your deceased parent gave you. Gratitude for all that they did to shape you. I owe Mum that.

*

Mothers sacrifice so much for their children and get little thanks for it. What shapes us, as mothers, is whether we're accepting of this truth or not. Mothers are adept at surrender. Or are expected to be. They begin our story. Shape it like no other. Elayn's determination to escape her predetermined destiny was the pathway for me to a world of books and writing. I was not to leave school early, not to be denied uni, not to marry a coalminer, not to disappear into a world of suburbia, not to be nibbled away at, the woman's lot. All, all, Elayn's gifts.

*

The sending off to Susie Elelman's Deportment Classes in Wollongong to walk with books on my head. The physical straightening of my bookworm's back with a curt, admonishing hand – 'stop slumping,' 'sit straight.' The personal business cards Elayn had printed up for my eighteenth birthday which I never used, I was too embarrassed. All this shaping helped me land a radio cadetship at the Australian Broadcasting Corporation because I'd learnt to elocute thanks to years of Verse Speaking Eisteddfods. My brothers speak differently, as if from another world; this was noted, wondrously, by various Sydneysiders at Elayn's funeral. I was the one hanging on by the coat-tails to the Great Acceleration. Yet from mid-teens onwards, there was no effusive gratitude. There was no passionate cry of 'I love you so much,' as I had at the morgue. If I could have one more minute of her, just one, I'd make amends.

*

Elayn was my anchor to a world of Home, and the point of resistance to be escaped from. The anchor to which I returned to five years ago after fifteen years in exile. Andrew and I had both loved the freedom of the expat's life because away you're the giddy cleanskin, whereas at home you can never completely escape your past. Away, you can reinvent yourself, do what you really want to do; be, finally, yourself – for you're not constantly judged and admonished by those close to you. The anonymity of the exile is exhilarating and liberating because away, you can step into your true self. I found that. So did Elayn.

Now she is gone. I am free of her, free of all of it. There is no need to be here anymore. I can go anywhere now, unanchored. The end is the start and I cannot bear it. Do not know where a belonging is anymore.

Need a skinful of new air. Need to hide. Disappear. Repair.

12

Several days later. Wandering through the flat. Paul and myself. Looking for clues, Elayn's mind frame, a sign. Any subtlety that the police may have missed. But nothing. No grand gesture. No last-minute tidying up, no hidden note just for us. So we search again. Like forensic detectives or debt collectors looking for something, anything, with assessing eyes; and this presses heavily upon us, that we are here, doing this. Struck, too, by how little is actually salvageable here. A lifetime of spectacular living, reduced to this. The flat was crammed with almost forty years of Elayn's world and now she is gone and it astonishes my brother and I how quickly an entire life can be silenced. Packed up, swept away, a fully lived existence reduced to a few boxes, if that.

It is bleak work. Weighted with sadness. We are not good at this.

*

Clothes, good clothes, hang on Elayn's cupboard door. Coffin clothes. Right. Yes. A sign, surely? Just one. Or is it? Elayn's signature red lipstick is on her dressing table as if left there in readiness, or perhaps as the daughter who'd observed Elayn's life I'm just instinctively stepping into her world here, her thinking. Learning her rhythms, habits, idiosyncrasies of home life, guessing them correctly because I'm a Chinese whisper of her.

*

Paul and I work swiftly, checking the kitchen cupboards and garage for perishables. Everything feels lonely now. Elayn loved a bargain and there are stacks and stacks of washing powder cartons and toilet paper packets that have been on special somewhere; waiting for a long future life, a future apocalypse, and now mocking us.

*

What is lost: Sunday roast dinners with their perfectly crunchy potatoes in duck fat that we've never been able to replicate. Elayn stopped doing big family meals in my late teens, couldn't wait to dive into another life, a released life. Yet forever onwards she carried the promise of those roast dinners. She did everything well, perfectly, including cooking; yet this doesn't mean she enjoyed it. Anything involving domestic life. The Chinese whisper, each to each: we both considered domesticity as time stolen from doing something else. A wider life.

*

What is lost: The anticipation of what Elayn would be wearing. It was often striking. Beautifully pressed. Accessorised with an extravagantly ruffled jacket, crisp collar, audacious necklace. There was always a pop of colour – usually red – and that increased most joyously with the encroaching years, as if to say 'I'm still here!' No slinking off into invisibility for this one. Her style was always instructive to others and myself, meticulously chosen, considered; a sign of inner vibrancy. One must never let oneself go. I was proud of her whenever she was introduced to friends or colleagues who didn't know her. I felt enhanced belonging to her. She was the cool mum.

*

Andrew and I and the kids had not been invited to this flat, as a family, at any time during the last five years of Elayn's life. I'd only been in it on and off, briefly, if a task needed doing.

Several years ago, Elayn was in hospital. A seizure had been triggered by an accidental overdose of the drug Thyroxin, which she took every day following the removal of her cancerous thyroid. She asked me to go into her flat and retrieve a phone charger.

It was the first time I'd been inside for a long, long time. There'd been many years of frustration about never being allowed back into my old teenage world, of resentment building up like silt, because she visited our house for dinner on a regular basis yet never reciprocated. I turned her house key in its familiar, tricky combination involving two locks and a gentle push, a procedure I'd known since my childhood years that was coming back to me as surely as riding a bicycle after decades. I pushed open the heavy door into a world I'd left for good at eighteen.

Sadness, above all. At piles of accumulations. Files and papers and boxes stacked in the lounge room, eating it up with neglect. At the ugly, fusty, patterned carpet that had been there for decades and even thirty-odd years ago had seemed burdened by too much dust. At three crowded bedrooms of endless, useless clothes; a lot never worn. At gaps where furniture had once been; the only sign of its absence indented markings on the carpet. What had Elayn been doing? Selling it?

Stains on the bathroom roof. Mould in a neglected ceiling corner. Faded furniture that had seen better days, imitation antiques that would never be anything but imitation antiques. It felt desolate, like an old lady hoarder's house. In an instant my thinking about my mother shifted, lifted. Into understanding. The knot of anger towards her softened into something else. Pity. It all felt so … lonely. Elayn wasn't being selfish or imperious or snobby by not allowing the rabble of my family near her world – she was being protective. Of herself.

*

On this gruelling morning of sifting and searching, Elayn's sewing room is a time capsule. Next to the old machine perches the wicker sewing box of mysterious entanglements and its companion, the tall button jar, packed to the rim with alluring samples of tweed and silk, velvet and ivory. I can see so clearly the curve of Elayn's concentrated back over the machine, making her creations. Can hear the pulse of its whirr, stopping and starting, an aural rhythm of absorbing work that my daughter will never know.

Elayn was always trying to change me with that machine. Designing a different girl's primary school uniform because she didn't like the fit of the official one. Copying kids' clothes in velvet and lace from the variety music show *Young Talent Time*. Organising tiny, plastic, serrated wheel-like attachments for my school shoe heels that forced my feet outwards and stopped me from being pigeon-toed. Forever tampering, moulding, bettering.

*

At seventeen, Elayn bought me a school formal dress. It was expensive, frilly, wrong. I couldn't tell her at the time it just wasn't me, I didn't want to crush her enthusiasm in the shop. Eventually, I made one myself. Sequins and chiffon, on her machine. I offered to pay for the one she bought me with my own pocket money. Looking back, my handmade effort was awful. But as always with Mum I had to do it my way. I wouldn't listen. Throughout her life Elayn had never experienced such thorough, consistent, rejection as from me, her daughter.

*

The fridge on this bleak morning is a snapshot of a life well preserved, crammed with monotonous health. Prunes and soy milk, cooked rice, fish ready for steaming, green vegetables, a carton of skinny milk I'd bought Elayn a week previously still tipped on its side, just as I'd left it, barely touched. She ate little in her final weeks, didn't get much enjoyment out of it. All appetite for living lost.

*

Some parents believe that if you want a child to do well you ignore them. Never give them praise or love, never throw them the juicy bone of attention. All my achievements feel like a scream to be noticed. Yet my mother would barb with cruelty. Quote back paragraphs to me of bad reviews for my books, word perfect; she had memorised the most cutting of phrases. Or talk about similar writers to myself with extravagant praise while pointedly saying nothing about a book of my own just out. Or say that she was going to write a book herself, it was easy, just wait. Beyond the sting of the hurt I assumed Elayn was a product of her generation. An Australia that didn't big-note or boast; that gleefully cut down its tall poppies. With pursed lips, she was making sure her daughter was kept in her place.

As we're going through the flat Paul and I find a box of clippings. My press. Twenty years' worth. Interviews and articles, many I've never seen before. I could never bear to look closely at any of it; it never felt really me; I usually hated the photos and was frustrated when misquoted or quoted out of context so hadn't been too bothered about collecting it all. Yet Elayn carefully cut out and catalogued a boxful of articles. She gave me a life's stretch of tut; when talking with me about my writing she was often suspicious, censorious, wary.

But then secretly, this.

Is there love here? Love is the gift of attention. *This* is attention. I take the box home for what it says about Elayn rather than me. She actually, deeply, cared. Oh.

*

Elayn is the embodiment of Proust's mother, who addled her son so potently by continually failing to climb the stairs to kiss him good night. And so I left, to pursue a writing life. Somewhere else, always somewhere else. Wanting anywhere but home.

Patrick White said, 'I knew more or less before I arrived that my mother and I could not live in the same hemisphere.' He said he always found that something positive, either creative or moral, came out of anything he experienced in the way of affliction. And so he wrote.

Being removed from Elayn's world was my fuel.

*

Paul and I retreat. A last sweep of the flat, checking that power switches are off and windows secured. The world of Elayn's home – her centre, her nest – is now lifeless. Waiting with breath held for the next person or people, whoever that may be. This is one of the last times my brother and I shall see all the familiar possessions we've known our entire lives; waiting forlornly now for dispersal, and forgetting. The shock of white secateurs from toddler days, even though Elayn hasn't had a garden for decades. A biscuit tin from the very first house we lived in, a modest white weatherboard barely altered even now. A desk with a map of the world on it that we both studied on. A Noritake tea set Elayn was so proud of, for so long, then just wanted to offload but never got around to it. Plastic biros from decades ago, no longer in shops. The flat reflects nothing of the dazzling public image so carefully cultivated. In this lair that is Elayn's real world, her life was closing over her. All around Paul and I are the humble accruals of a little, elderly, exhausted life. That no one else would want. Including us.

*

Taken, Elayn's scarves. Fifty or so. She had many, in a blare of brightness, to cover the surgical scar on her throat. The scarves smell thickly of her as do her clothes, smell of her washing powder and White Linen perfume. I open her cupboard and breathe deep. Oh to bottle that smell.

A while ago, at a funeral, I'd seen each church pew draped with a woman's lifetime of scarves, and all the congregation was invited to take one home as a memory at the service's end. I'd spoken to Elayn of this at the time and she thought it a grand idea. We had no idea that the gesture would be used at her own funeral just a few, fragile months later.

*

The secret loneliness of Elayn's flat. Her motto through life: 'If I rest, I rust.' She knew that with rupture we're always learning something new, if we're open to it, and she was courageously unafraid of change. Except when it

113

came to this, her flat. The disconnect between public and private is almost violent. Many acquaintances knew only the vivacious woman who seized life; who loved her theatre and film and writers' festivals and travel. Few knew the other woman, prone to depression, alone in her stale flat. And in the end this world won. It swallowed her up.

*

Paul and I need repairing threads of gold to put us right, here, now. With our mother's presence filling out these rooms there had been a transformation of the ordinary; everything had a story, a preciousness. With Elayn gone her possessions hold no allure. They languish unwanted, unclaimed. Everything feels abandoned now.

What to do with all the photos of strangers – at functions, on South Pacific cruises, cradling unrecognised babies. It feels like sacrilege to ditch them. All those lives, treasured by someone; yet Paul and I leave them for someone else and walk away from this desolate place with heavy, inadequate hearts.

We're no good at this.

13

Officialdom is not asking for access to Elayn's body – it's declaring it.

Paul and I do not fight the autopsy ruling; we have no fight left in us, over anything. We need closure too, need our uncertainties erased. The procedure will be invasive. Our mother will be dramatically cut open. To soften the blow, perhaps, we're told that the doctor wants to check if our mother's cancer had come back. If this, possibly, was a cause of her anguish.

In the world of inconclusive death and police procedurals, things move fast; the autopsy is to be performed the day after the coroner's request. T, our familiar counsellor from the morgue, is sympathetic but clear on the phone: this may provide answers but it may not, that is the way of these things. We have to be prepared. She the protector, shadowing our grief.

*

One question hovering above all: Elayn robbed us of a mother – or did she? Paul and I still hope, somehow, that it was an accident. A deliberate choice is just too rejecting.

*

The funeral. Have to get on to it. People pressing us, time pressing us; she can't stay refrigerated in that crammed morgue forever. Paul suggests a firm staffed by women. 'So Elayn.' One that promises the Australian way of death, with a woman's touch. Attendants wear white jackets and smart hats at the service. It's exactly how Mum would have wanted it; a panoply of strong, efficient, organised, appreciative women to send her off.

The funeral director, G, is older, motherly. Over a cup of tea the grief cannot be contained, she pushes a tissue box towards me. She understands, has seen it all, will get me through this. Paul is back in Newcastle but on speakerphone. I select the wood of the coffin like we're selecting kitchen cupboards. There'll be speeches and poems, the vibe will be vibrant, the colours of the flowers youthful and bright. All, so very, Elayn.

*

I shy away from volunteering to dress my mother. I cannot imagine seeing her without clothes. Her body has revolted me ever since I saw it naked, often as a teenager, as she'd wander around the flat with no clothes on, doing her hair and makeup, organising herself. I do not want to see the ravages of the autopsy, nor revisit the unearthly coldness of her flesh all over again. I selected Elayn's funeral clothes as if she was going to a wedding. The good clothes from her cupboard door, the bra among her satiny best, underpants pristine, shoes polished. Am glad it will be G doing this intimate women's business, that I know her.

Elayn will travel from the church service to the crematorium without us. We'll farewell her at the church. A collective decision. Not sure if it's right. G assures me it happens a lot now; that the crematorium is very far away, through heavy traffic, it's an anticlimax after the service, the cars lose their tight processional order as others cut in. I worry that Elayn will be alone for her final hour on this earth. Without us. Still, she chose lonely, at the end.

*

Ticky's high school rings in the thick of the funeral arranging. It's his house tutor, who oversees his pastoral care. My eldest has come into her office and broken down. 'What happened to my nonna,' he has cried. 'Why were the police involved? Was she murdered?' The school has umbrellaed us with their concern since I told his house tutor of the death after the police had left my house on the Friday,

118

while the boys were still at school. Ticky's housemaster had rung me at home on the Saturday morning and again on the Sunday night, to see how both sons were travelling, how we all were travelling. The moving kindness. And now this.

The school tells me that Ticky needs help. As soon as possible. They have a counsellor on tap; I had no idea. They want my poor, bewildered, broken boy to see her as soon as possible, today, this lunchtime if possible. It's that urgent. But she wants to speak to me first.

*

Breaking, afresh. Cannot hold the pieces of all my family together. Explaining through new tears to C, the school counsellor, that we haven't yet told the boys their beloved Nonna may have killed herself. Only that Nonna died in her sleep. We don't know the cause yet. I tell C I'm not sure how long I can keep the story up. Until this point our house has been a leaden mix of lowered voices when children enter the room; of clamming up and shutting down, lowered eyes and evasion. But Nonna Chose to Leave Us? It's too momentous right now. Too blunt.

*

'You have to tell Ticky the truth,' C counsels. 'And your thirteen year old. If you don't, they'll find out eventually.

And they'll be so angry at you for lying to them, for not treating them as adults. They'll hate you for it. Grieve all over again, which means they'll be grieving twice.'

Yet what, exactly, is the truth here? Everyone seems to be assuming something my brother and I are not, just yet. Or can't face. Head cram, too much. I explain to C that our family isn't into therapists, have never had a need of one; we aren't against them in any way, just aren't used to them. She says Ticky needs to see her. The school wants him to. It needs my permission.

I give it. C won't tell him anything specific, she'll leave this to me. 'But I'm worried – and it's ridiculous, I know – that their lives will somehow be stained by knowing that there's a suicide in the family. That in some awful moment of anger, some silly, mindless fit of teenage angst, they might run outside and do something stupid like throw themselves off a cliff.'

C tells me teenagers are affected by the suicide of their peers, but it's a different story with older people around them. They're not a trigger in the way the copycat suicides of teens can be. G, the funeral director, concurs. My boys have to be told. She's been in enough situations to know they're old enough and can take it. They'll deal with it in their own way.

*

And then like some ridiculous farce of too-muchness, in the midst of all this the coroner's assistant, T, calls.

It is done. The model's body dissected. Would Elayn have known this invasive autopsy would be happening to her, as a consequence of how she died? Results, I am told, are 'pending'. Won't be known for a month or months. G had told me this is the case in ninety per cent of autopsies. So, still no definitive answer. 'Can you tell me anything?' I plead to T.

'The doctor did say that your mother had the most unbelievably healthy internal organs.' I think of Elayn's fridge crammed with all its fashionable health; its rice and fish and quinoa and prunes. 'He had never seen such splendid ones in someone her age. They were incredibly well preserved.' So. Several more decades left in her. Right. Her mother had lived to one hundred and Elayn could have done that too.

'I shouldn't tell you this,' T adds, 'but the doctor did remark that she had the most beautiful aorta he'd ever seen.' Of course. Even internally Elayn was physically dazzling. All this well-intentioned detail is all the more heartbreaking. The waste. Of a good, healthy, vibrant life. 'There was no cancer,' T adds. 'But the doctor did say that he could tell from your mother's feet that she had been in a lot of pain. There was also scoliosis of the spine.'

Oh Mum. That her final months were so weighted with all that. Scoliosis, the twisted spine, the crippling disease

121

that teenagers get and none of us knew. But it was in her walk in her final weeks. In her body twisted in agony around a walking stick. In my memory of a mother who seemed suddenly shrunk to almost half her height.

*

C, the counsellor, rings after lunch. It's been a good session. 'He's such a beautiful boy.' I know, oh I know, and I'm fighting my hardest to keep him that way.

*

The teenage boys arrive home from school earlier than the little ones. We tumble into our extravagantly oversized armchair that can accommodate all three of us. I hold them, stroke them, breathe them in deep, just like I used to when they were toddlers. They do not resist, rare at this age. Deep breath. Time for the truth. That Nonna may have overdosed accidently on her painkillers. That she had spoken of the agony to them, remember, had been hobbling and twisted in this very room. But it's more likely that she possibly, perhaps, took her own life.

A pause. The boys absorb it. Many questions. They sense a narrative taking shape. Clarity trickles into their thinking. It feels like something has lifted between us. The air has cleared. As we talk, adult to adult. For what feels like the first time in our lives. Adult concepts, adult ways. Our relationship has shifted into a different plane. The counsellor was right.

*

That night, in Ticky's eyes, a knowledge that he has entered some grown-up world of limitless complication. A world of pain and sadness, failure and despair that he has never, deeply, known. But he can take it. The resilience of the young. Something within him is repairing, moving on. He wants to see the school counsellor again tomorrow. Threads of repairing gold.

*

But Elayn. All the complexity she has left us with. What bleakly adult world have the children been plunged into with their grandmother's flinty choice?

14

Yet at the same time as the loss, there is a freeing. From silences. From attack. From the exhaustion of never knowing what would be coming at you – fulsome love or its withery opposite. From the extravagance of Elayn's emotions, whatever they were. As after the eviscerating words would come the wounded coiling into silence when it felt like something fundamental in life had been severed. It is a bitter truth: you hurt those you love the most, because you know them too well. You hurt them with vicious effectiveness.

*

Elayn wanted the perfect daughter. Beautiful, quiet, talented, successful, pliant. The daughter wanted the perfect mother. Loving, generous, nurturing, understanding, forgiving. Perfection undid us, the expectation of it, the pursuit. We both had to be taught how to love with acceptance, looseness, forgiveness. The tragedy is, we were getting there.

*

When I was young Elayn would fling, 'No one likes you.' When I craved prettiness, 'You're so ugly.' When I didn't measure up in terms of a daughter, 'Why can't you be like M and O? I wish they were my daughters.' I was nine. She was referring to the prettiest and most popular girls in the class. It was like a tic of envy in her head. She wanted them but she had me, vined to her. Her swotty clod of a thing. That could write.

*

Elayn was always waiting when it came to a daughter. For me to bloom into prettiness. For me to become famous, which meant a specific type of adulation to do with television and television alone; the pinnacle was to have her daughter on the small screen in some revered journalistic capacity. She was waiting for gratitude. For her daughter to declare to the world that Elayn Gemmell was the person who made her, above all, and who she loved more than anyone, particularly her lowlife father. It didn't happen. This book could be it. Well, the gratitude bit.

*

All Elayn's frustration would spill out in her combing of my hair during the primary school years, tugging and yanking and pulling at my knots. It hurt, physically and emotionally, it bewildered me. All that anger in a brush stroke. As a consequence, I do not touch my daughter's hair. Sometimes, wilfully, you live your adult life in opposition to how you were parented. You evolve. Most determinedly, you evolve.

*

Some friends have mothers capable of immense cruelty. Friends who weep all the way home in their car after a visit. Who've sought divorce counselling from their mother because it's just too hard to be with them. Who've had to move to a new state to remove themselves from the destructive, narcissistic press of the woman who gave birth to them. Who haven't spoken to their mother for years, even as grandchildren have arrived. Just to survive.

My friends and I wonder about these perplexing women of the fifties, snagged by frustration and taking it out on daughters who live so differently to them. They came of age pre-feminism and we came of age post-feminism and sometimes the gulf feels too far to bridge. We have opportunities they never had. Yet it doesn't seem to make them celebratory, it makes them bitter.

*

'Hi Mum.' A light, breezy 'Hi Nik' in return on the phone was rare. The cool 'Hello Nikki' more common. Sometimes, a long pause, then a weary 'Hello.' Just that. The tormenting of silence. Most times there was a knot in my stomach when calling her. Because I never knew what mother I'd get.

But I was always the one to apologise. Even when I wasn't sure what for. Sorry wasn't in Elayn's vocabulary when it came to her daughter.

*

'The knowledge that she would never be loved in return acted upon her ideas as a tide acts upon cliffs,' wrote Thornton Wilder in *The Bridge of San Luis Rey*. Always, always, the little girl, desperate for scraps of affirmation. Even into middle age. And when it came, the euphoria, leaving me craving more.

'He who loves the most is the inferior and must suffer,' Thomas Mann wrote. In my case, I loved the most because I was the child. Always the child, with Elayn, needing affirmation.

*

Sometimes family is not a gift but an endurance. And sometimes, to endure, you have to distance yourself from it. That's why so many of my adult years were spent living away from family. A lot of the time I couldn't endure my mother. Yet in her last five years I came home. To find a suturing. To make it work. To prove it could be done. I'd have gone mad, now, if I hadn't done that.

*

Freed from: Elayn's game, year after year, when my birthday was held hostage to whether I was in her good books or not, demonstrated by whether I'd be rung or not. If I was in favour she'd lavish me with love; a beautifully worded card and an exquisitely wrapped present. Gift wrapping, for Elayn, fell under her remit of perfection; every paper selection and ribbon had to be just so. On the last birthday I spent with her it was all this, fulsomely. We had a lunch in the Members Dining Room of State Parliament. She worked there as a casual receptionist to the politicians of New South Wales and loved their imposing, clubby environs of privilege and poshness. I was issued a security pass and met her colleagues; it was a tsunami of care and attention. I remain stunned. Perhaps we were both changing.

At the end of the lunch, Elayn broke the news that she was going into hospital for a foot operation in the next few weeks, and might need some help.

*

Most often, during my adult birthdays, there was only vicious silence. No call, no acknowledgment. This would stain whatever festivities I was having on the day with a fuming at the game of withholding. Elayn's birthday was four months after mine. Each year, after yet another great silence, I'd think no, I'm not going to contact her, she needs a taste of her own medicine. And each year as Elayn's birthday came around I'd soften, call, give a gift. Couldn't bear to sink to her level. Couldn't bear the admission of my own littleness, alongside her, in the depths.

*

'What to do with her, with the hostility, undying, which I feel for her? I want, as ever, to grab my life from out under her hot, itchy hands. My life, my writing, my husband, my unconceived baby. She's a killer, watch out …' Sylvia Plath on her mother. My mother propelled me into writing. Into a different kind of life. Far removed from her world, from everything she stood for. I knew it at fifteen as a judging teenager and I know it now, deep in motherhood.

Elayn did not fully grasp the consequences of what she was doing. Does any parent? She underestimated my anger at being pushed in directions I did not want to go in; at being forced to be someone I wasn't comfortable being. And by pushing me, actually, into another life, so different to Elayn's, I would always, somehow, be beyond her. Did she hate and admire this at the same time? There is the riddle of painstakingly curated clippings, yet the attempts to my face to constantly reduce me for my choices; put me in my place.

What I've learnt: that as a parent, we cannot rigidly shape our children's lives no matter how much we would like to. We have to step back and watch them bloom into who they are meant to be, whether we like it or not. We have to step back with understanding, and love.

*

Once Elayn walked suddenly into my teenage room (just as she used to when I was child, just as she always would) and came upon a canvas flung across the floor. All my anger and frustration and torment was spilled out in the vicious colour, the furious strokes. She said – bewildered, serious, weary – 'Sometimes I wonder what I've raised.' As if I was not quite human. Not part of her known world. And she really didn't want to have to deal with it.

*

And yet, and yet … I miss her wisdom. The talks about men. On N, the fiancé who jilted me: 'Look at his girlfriends, his past. Why is he still so friendly with all of them? If you love someone that deeply, and it falls apart, you cannot bear to look at them.' She said that maybe all it needed was six months, and perhaps he would come back the better man: 'If it's true love it will still be there. And it'll be mature love then.'

Of an early boss, summed up from one handshake: 'He lacks confidence. He lives under the shadow of his parents. He'd be clingy and needy if you were in a relationship with him. He'd chip away at you to reduce you, bring you down to his level.'

Of an ex-boyfriend: 'He's quite charming in his unsophistication.' And that was on a good day.

'Beware the controlling man. Don't ever get caught up with one. They'll destroy you.' This one on my wedding eve, yet I was able to soothe Elayn that she had no fear on that score. She didn't know Andrew beyond his beautiful voice; didn't know how comfortable he was in his own skin. Didn't know I'd learnt from her.

*

'Don't sell your flat.' Mum never wanted me to get rid of my old, single woman's flat, in Sydney's Kings Cross, to have it subsumed by marital finances. To her it represented financial freedom. An escape if ever it was needed. She'd worked hard after her divorce to pay off the mortgage on her newly acquired flat and wanted her daughter to have that surety too. Independence, especially within a marriage. A way out, just in case. On my wedding day she walked me down the aisle as the proud single woman who'd raised me, while my father stood beside us in the pew. My grandmother, Lexi, was so appalled she refused to go to the wedding. Bob was fine with it. He knew the truth of the situation.

*

I moved briefly home when I was eighteen, between house shares. Elayn let the boy who took my virginity stay in my tiny childhood bedroom with its high, narrow bed; happy for him to invade my little-girl world. When I lost my virginity she was celebratory and brisk. Ordered me to see a doctor, to get the pill quickly. That feeling of horror, as a teenager, that now I would be like her. All … appetite.

*

I didn't tell Elayn when I got my first period. Denying her this seminal, mother–daughter moment. I had to work out how to insert the tampon myself, and wondered if I'd found the right hole. Distance, and removal.

*

When I became engaged to N I was living in Alice Springs, Elayn in Sydney. I told her over the phone we were getting married. It was fine, she was happy. But then a night of reflection. The next day, the tone in her voice, the judgment. I said that L, a journalist, had managed to get him and I tickets to the Sydney Film Festival's opening night. This did not change her stance. The sing-song, accusatory, 'What are you wearing? We dress smartly in Sydney you know. You don't want to look like an Alice Springs waif.' I loved my mother. I did not like her.

*

Yet I wanted the children to have her in their lives; to know the solace of a Nonna because I'd had two guiding grandmotherly lights. Andrew and I had made the decision to return home from London to reconnect with our blood and land and hearts. For our children to connect too. To know their Nonna in ways far richer than made possible by her trips to England every couple of years, or our crammed visits back home when there were always too many people in too few days.

*

As the days lurch on, the weeping. That Elayn did not love my children so much that she wanted to see them grow up, was not fuelled by curiosity. Did the kids sense it at all? She would sit in the car rather than walk inside with me

133

to collect Jages from his preschool, choosing not to revel in seeing him in his happy school environment; she would bow out of invitations to the older kids' presentation days with a dismissive 'I'm busy.' Her incuriosity was striking. Did she love any of us, enough? We could not hold her in this world, not a single one of us.

*

I wish for Elayn now a different life. We – her children – held her back, exhausted her. I wish for her now a university education, a continuation of her modelling career, a flowering into the world of business. My father didn't want a wider world for her, with other men, and Elayn surrendered. Shortly after they divorced Bob married a woman nineteen years younger than him. She was everything Elayn wasn't. Fervent with domesticity, proud to be a traditional homemaker. Swiftly they had four children. It was a much more solid match. I've grown to love my stepmother. To appreciate all she's done for my father in making him settled and happy. But for a while there, during my teen years, I was bewildered by the vast loneliness she made me feel within the family she had created with my dad. The obscenity of that. Yet did I ever consider that I made Elayn lonely within her family?

*

In the seventies, when my parents divorced, a fractured family wasn't called a single parent family, with all the strength that that entails. It was a broken home. That's what I came from. And it felt broken, our family unit, all five of us. It still does. Yet to me the words single mum and feminist always seem to go together. You can't have one without the strength of the other.

Elayn always acted with audacity. Unlike my stepmother, who made the better wife.

*

Elayn could not bring herself to say Bob's name without her voice souring with hate. 'Your father.' The ugly spit of it never changed. We'd spoken of Bob briefly before Ticky's birthday dinner, driving to the restaurant; he was coming down soon from his country home to look after the kids because Andrew and I had an interstate wedding. 'Your father.' The hrumph of contempt. No-good lump of a thing, her voice conveyed, just as it had when I was ten.

*

'Tell your father your maintenance is due.' 'Get the towels, bitch.' 'No one likes you.' 'I wish I had _____ as my daughter, not you.' Elayn made me feel grubby, grubby I couldn't get rid of. She was hard as a door banging on your fingers at times. Her death was not a happy, light one. Her lonely choice reflected the sadness in her life.

*

Elayn had never, once, offered to look after my children in the five years I'd been home. I'd asked a few times but it was always 'I'm busy' in response so I soon learnt to stop. We were living down the road but it was not in her DNA to provide assistance. It took me years to understand this. That she had done her dash with her own children, that she wanted to live her own life now, that young children were depleting. Bob is the opposite – regularly helps, despite living a day's travel away. He'll bound into Jages' preschool to help me pick him up, delighting in gazing at his grandson in his world. As a parent, I couldn't help but veer to that. Elayn was unable to cut through our father–daughter bond, and she hated it. For four decades I endured her hatred of it.

*

Working side by side with my father, securing a new hammock between palm trees. 'You know,' Bob commented, 'in all my years of marriage to your mother she never once lifted a hand to help me.' I tell him it was the same for me, and with Win, her mother. Building up the

136

walls around herself until at last, in her final act, she was alone. Her choice.

*

Elayn resented my love for my father after they divorced. I was ten. I was not meant to love him after they had split up; I was expected to hate him as much as she did. No idea why. In my late teens I wrote a piece about my father's and grandfather's coalmining lives, which was published in the literary magazine *Quadrant*. The commissioning editor and poet, Les Murray, wrote in his letter of offer, 'If you made this up, you're a genius.' I didn't.

Elayn was so angry after she read the essay. I was confused because this was one of my first pieces of published writing; the catapult into the dream. I'd finally cracked it. Yet this was Elayn's response: How dare I express a love of my father in print. How dare I commit that love to permanence. How dare I mention his coalmining background; the world she escaped from and never mentioned socially. How dare I let the cat out of the bag, in her new, severed life that was removed from all of that.

*

Elayn's powerful, blunt hands. They could open any jar with a fiercely effective, almost superhuman twist. City hands, of course, with their red nails and elaborate rings, but hands that shouted a robust bush past. I envied them.

*

Elayn was a woman made strong by her own suffering. Like *Kintsugi*, she was shaped by the dents and the cracks. Throughout all the twists and turns of life, the setbacks and the humiliations, she wanted me to be that woman too.

*

I left Elayn, emotionally, at thirteen, when she forced me to buy my own school shoes to teach my father a lesson because his maintenance payment was late. Flinty rage, as I caught the bus to the shopping centre with a purse full of birthday money. Flinty rage, at being used as a pawn in someone else's war. Flinty rage, poured into my teenage journal. Yet her lessons grew me up.

*

My Snoopy diary, aged fourteen, records Elayn saying that no one would care if I died, that I was a slut, a slob. As a shy convent girl I didn't know boys throughout my entire high school years; not until first year university, aged eighteen.

Her rage came from a dark, deep place I had no access to. It felt immoral. Still does.

*

The sense of responsibility changed. For Elayn, for us. As she aged I was now looking after her. It was draining and exhausting but right. She was in her mid-sixties, it was time for me to step up. Give back. While she was in London and staying with us I was checking bus timetables, cooking for her, opening cans for her, putting on her music. She was to be waited upon. It was like she had completely given up; or decided that her time was due. That she had spent her whole adult life giving and giving, as a wife and mother, and now it was time to get something back. I did it because I knew it to be so.

*

When I visited Sydney with my eldest, baby Ticky, Elayn didn't want us to stay. She said it would be 'too stressful'. She didn't touch him on that first visit. Eventually, over time, she held him, but was always quick to hand him back if he was squally or restless. At the time, this felt not only a rejection of me but my baby, my first child.

Theories from various people:

139

Elayn was just not a baby person.

She had lived by herself for so long she had locked herself within selfishness.

She was having difficulty coming to terms with being a grandmother; it aged her; the former model whose dazzling youthfulness had carried her through life.

She didn't want any more hurt from me.

She was afraid. 'It's been thirty-five years since I've done this,' she had said to an old friend, the mother of A, my best friend, as they were changing Ticky's nappy together.

She had no idea how I'd cope with being a mother and thought perhaps I wouldn't; that I'd lean on her too much for support.

My theory: all of the above. And that she was afraid of being shown up.

*

Elayn would have been a fabulous, childless, career woman. She had always been a sexy woman because she looked like she revelled in life; looked like a woman who loved laughing in bed. There was a succession of boyfriends during my teenage years. Sunday outings on the harbour in their boats, trips to bush weekenders. I always felt I failed her; the studious, shy teen with the greasy hair and spots, blushing with my awkwardness. The teen with the glamorous mother who'd swim with her boyfriend in the bush in just her underpants, who'd honk the car horn at the black sailors when the American warships were in town. Who was so exasperated when I put on my first pair of reading glasses; that I'd slithered into this strange, nerdy world; that I'd become so other.

*

At the end of her life Elayn lost her sense of joy. Pain crushed out everything that had characterised her. Optimism, independence, vibrancy, audacity, glee.

*

Elayn and I were the only two females of the family and should have been allies. We never were. It was more competitive than that; about allegiances, with my father most of all. My raw, wounded soul, too big and hurting for all this; years and years of aching soul. Because mothers weren't meant to be like this.

*

She never said I love you. Even in her final email couldn't bring herself to say it. Perhaps she felt it would reduce her, diminish her. Cause her to cede, just a touch, a cherished sense of control.

Our entire life together, as mother and daughter: a battle for control.

*

Stories start here, in the abandonment of the child by the parent, in the pulling away of the child from the mother. My journals only record the hurting times because stories inherently seek drama. But there were bounteous times too, and I have not recorded those. As Philip Larkin wrote, 'What will survive of us is love', and I have to hold on to that. Non-fiction is never as neat as fiction. There is so much that is inexplicable, that doesn't follow known patterns, that trips up and surprises. Elayn had the capacity to buoy me like no other person. That was her secret and her power. And she did, oh she did. All it took was the gift of attention.

*

I couldn't understand the tricks and barbs of a maternal terrorist. And then, of course, she'd come back. Like my last birthday with her, when she asked me to be there for her during the foot operation. And I was, of course I was. To be needed is a fundamental human desire.

*

Whatever happens with my own children, I never want them to be unsure of my love. Elayn was not so vigilant. 'I raised you in the Dr Spock era,' she told me once, as if by way of apology, 'it was different then.' Doris Lessing wrote of her mother, 'We were engaged in bitter warfare all the time.' Elayn and I didn't have the relentlessness of that, there were periods of great mateship, but we were two strong women battling for ascendency. Yet I loved her too much during the fraught times to let her go entirely. Do problematic mothers brew writers? The anger that first flint into finding your voice. But I am conscious of the fact that this book only tells one side of a story, as women have so often only told one side of this story. Simone de Beauvoir, Helen Garner, Germaine Greer, Miles Franklin, Marguerite Duras, Elena Ferrante.

*

Paul thinks Elayn suffered from depression on and off throughout her life. That she would have been a different woman – would have parented differently – if Prozac had been available in the sixties and seventies. And we all would have had different lives.

*

I was scared to come too close to her. My mother bewildered me. But mothers aren't meant to do that. Our

143

adult relationship, for much of it, could be described as 'thinness'. Thinness of coming together, thinness of bonding, a tragedy of thinness.

*

I struggle to write, for months after the death. Columns, novel, this book, anything. It feels like Elayn has hijacked me. I can no longer work like I used to. She was never sure of my writing and this felling, now, feels deliberate. I struggle to find cohesion, unable to piece anything together, losing flow. Failing, falling.

*

I'd always mute myself with apology. Didn't have it in me to attack with that most wounding weapon of all, silence. With her final act Elayn has destroyed me. I fought for so long not to have her get to me. She has triumphed. I have lost. I am blindsided.

By love.

15

An elderly woman's fear of nursing homes. A model's fear of aging and all its irreversible failings. Elayn rarely visited her own mother, Win, when she was placed in a home in her late nineties. I had put Win there, along with my two brothers and Win's daughter-in-law. We were tasked with determining her care as Elayn wanted nothing to do with it. And so Winnifred McNee, the Barnardos child who went on to be a jillaroo, nanny and lift operator in an exuberantly lived life, did not go gentle into that good home. And suddenly, after a lifetime of chuff towards her grandchildren, there was anger. How did it come to this?

*

Win was born in London's East End while her mother was in service. Her mother struggled to raise her and when Win was five she sent her off to a children's home in Hackney. Aged eleven, Win was shipped across the world to Western Australia's Fairbridge Farm School. She hauled herself away from the expectations of the powers that be – that she was destined for a life of domestic service – by using a fine mind and an inclusive sociability. After two husbands, three children and varied, satisfying work she found herself alone, deliciously, in her own flat, purchased from hard-earned funds; the one thing to show for a life fully lived.

Yet in Win's final years, she often returned to that sense of bewilderment she felt as a child. She couldn't release the past, and suddenly her beloved grandchildren were reminding her of it most cruelly with their actions. Because at the very end of her life we were putting her back in an institutional home. From ninety-eight onwards she had been in hospital a lot. Could barely get out of bed by herself, struggled to dress and shower; her mind was sparky but the body failing. 'There's no dignity in getting old, Nik.' During a lengthy hospital bout, mainly for constipation, medical staff told us it was time for a nursing home – Win could no longer use the hospital as a nursing facility. She indicated to all of us that yes, it was time.

But the day before Win was due to go into the home: nightmare, she dug in her heels. Snapped that she didn't want it, we weren't listening. The hospital called a family conference; all the way through it Win covered her ears, crying out, 'Stop talking, too loud, all of you.' The mess of it. Over days, weeks. Doctors and social workers explained she couldn't go back to her flat; Win had reached a critical stage in her care regime and needed a lot of help. We family members were swamped, couldn't think straight, wanted to do the right thing by Win but also her carers. I was shovelling baby mush into a stunned five year old's mouth and only realising my mistake when I caught my daughter's expression; the food was meant for her little brother. Elayn had no idea of the enormity of the stress the rest of us were under; she kept her distance. But she was hearing dribs and drabs. Dreading no doubt the moment when her time, too, would come. Like this.

*

What was learnt: That extreme stress, at any age, can be caused by a loss of control. Win had lost control of her life. Momentous decisions were being made without her say. What was also learnt: that strong, intelligent women can still be pleasers, right up until the end. As people in medical coats started suggesting a nursing home, Win acquiesced out of a sense of duty, but it was only when push came to shove that the enormity of the situation hit. And a submerged anger over a loss of control burst to the surface.

*

Win went off to her nursing home. We told her it was just for a month, a respite situation, because we couldn't bear to see her unhappy. If she still wanted to go home after that we'd do our best, with professional help. (I'd offered to have her with me: 'Only if you can give me a flat, Nik.' Wise words – I wouldn't have wanted to be crammed in with the mad, cacophonous lot of us either.) But as a woman whose early years were blighted by institutions she deserved a choice; she'd stayed active her entire life and we all dreaded the stasis of a nursing home. Of what it might do to her.

I felt like a failure. As a feminist, a woman, a granddaughter. Because an elderly female had declared she wanted to remain in her hard-earned flat for the rest of her life yet here she was now, in a nursing home. In a process of traumatic rupture. At ninety-nine.

*

Our family's lives were hijacked for months because we cared deeply about Win's wishes. Yet it was all becoming too vexingly complicated. How to respect the fierce independence? I recognised it, championed it. Knew it would keep her alive. Both of us dreaded the idea of a nursing home, a holding pen to death, where all control and choice is stripped from you. The institution we eventually admitted our beloved Win to, after weeks of research, had a 'high dependency unit' and it was a shock to pad through it on our way to her. The silence of the patients, the faces of ruined stillness, the staring

148

into space, the endless television seemingly unwatched. All those unvisited hours, all those days ticking by. The modern way of death.

*

But Win wasn't in that section. She was in a room of her own that she quickly made her own. She had lived an impressively active life of hard work, community service, tennis into her nineties and her giggly secret, a shot of brandy every night, and after several weeks in her new environment the question of returning to her flat became, miraculously, redundant. She was getting in-house care for relatively simple things that had hospitalised her previously. Head massages, hair care, day trips, tai chi. After several weeks of dipping in her toes, she plunged. Didn't looked back. It became hard to track her down when I phoned – she was never in her room. What to call her when I rang reception: client, patient, inmate? Our family referred to the place, jokingly, as 'the hotel', so it was 'guest.'

Peace of mind at last. That Win was not spending lonely days of nothing-much in her flat, staring at the telly; or worse, that she'd fallen and blacked out by herself. The low-level hum of worry – it had become a constant feature of our lives – was gone. We were all released.

*

What was learnt back then: If we let go and embrace change it can take us to unexpected places, like acceptance, discovery, delight, even at the age of ninety-nine. Eugène Ionesco spoke of the power of replenishment: 'there has always been at every living moment of culture a "will to renewal" … all history is nothing but a succession of "crises", of rupture.' Win had her own triumphant moment of renewal by surrendering to the unknown. At her one hundredth birthday party she looked healthy, engaged, present. She hadn't looked like that in the last months in her own flat; she had looked pale, ill and painfully thin because she wasn't eating enough. Yet Elayn had missed much of this journey.

*

As a daughter I get that you're sometimes screaming inside to disconnect, yet I remain shocked that Elayn spent so little time with Win in her final years.

Of course, as a mother you're sometimes screaming inside to disconnect too. Reclaim something of yourself. But now, with my own little brood, there's a determination not to repeat vexatious patterns of family-ing.

For example, my request to them all was modest: a Mother's Day sleep party. By myself, in a nearby hotel, to have one night of the deep, replenishing alone, after years of not. 'Can I come too?' my bouncy Biahbi, aged six, had asked. Gently I explained a sleep party involved me, a bed and no one else – for a very long time. Cue anguish, tears, confusion. Mummy, all by herself? At a party my daughter's not invited to? And she's the one who sleeps jammed up against me whenever she can, limpet-stuck, as if it's the only way she can sleep, as if she'll never let me go.

But she must at some point, of course, and how I dread it; dread it with all of them. Yet mothers let go too, some viciously. I've seen parents and children living in horror of each other's potency, each side knowing the other's Achilles heel too well. Yet I think of the urgency in W.H. Auden's plea, 'We must love one another or die,' for with those great familial silences, surely the most bitterest rifts of all, can come a sapping of the spirit, a corrosive bewilderment, a heaviness that's carried through life. You can't be hurt by someone you don't care about. And so Biahbi came with me. And so a sleepless night of wriggling and jiggling, elbows in the head and stolen blankets. We both loved it. Have done it often since.

*

No mother is perfect. No child. As parents we have to use our power wisely, with restraint and empathy. Sometimes it's bloody hard. Sometimes I feel more childish, less restrained than my kids; that they're better people than me. Motherhood is all-consuming, a condition of giving, continually. The love is voluminous, extravagant, greedy; it varnishes with light, it dulls; has me dancing around the room with exhilaration then exhausted on the ground, fists pressed at thudding temples, lost. And no matter how much love mothers have to give we're sometimes screaming inside for alone. To unfurl, to replenish.

That's why I'm always hoping for a sleep party. Sometimes insist to the children that I need one, alone. It won't last for long, just a night or two. And then the tribe will all come gleefully tumbling back into my world and I'll gather the small, bright wonder of them close and breathe them in deep. And when they leave in adulthood this giggle palace of a house will wait for them, breath held, as I too will wait. For the gift of their attention. For their understanding love. Despite all the faults.

16

Everywhere, as the funeral is organised, little biting reminders.

Ordering new glasses, the optometrist brings up Elayn's details rather than mine on his screen. 'My mother has died.' Can't bring myself to use the ugliness of that term 'passed'. Passed by, or through, what? After the insincere platitudes the optometrist goes back to his records. Types in laborious capital letters, DECEASED. The arresting baldness of it, still.

She is in her old shopping haunts, on her street, in the outline of a bowed body as a plate glass window is passed, in the curve of a wrist as I buy a new watchband, in the flowers and cards still coming in. My face is souring with the shock, my skin has lost buoyancy, it drops in despondency as does my step. I share her age spots, her smile, her clearing of the throat. She is taking over. I walk barefoot now, a lot; trying to thwart destiny's insistence, to veer my feet's fate. An excruciating pain curdles in my right hip. I know it's caused by stress and tension, but it's as if Elayn is haunting me: see, now you know chronic pain. Now you will understand. Pain's vice tightens.

*

A migraine holds normality hostage. Then another. As a teenager there were Saturday mornings of Elayn in bed; the blinds drawn, a flannel over the forehead, a face set in pain. Now it is my turn. One of our last conversations was about migraines. She said hers vanished after the change swept through her life at fifty-two. I, no doubt, will mirror that. So alike, so apart.

*

Through it all life goes on. From decades ago Elayn's friends are tracked down to break the news of death, then details of the funeral. The shock, the questions, the tears. Friends from Elayn's Wollongong world, her Hunter Valley world, her multiple working worlds. She was good at seeding, reaping, nourishing mateship. Always punctual, a sign of respect; and rarely letting mates down with commitments. A lot talk of her cards; the beautiful, cursive writing. Elayn existed richly in a world apart from her children; we're only realising the extent of it in her death. Many express guilt at not calling her in her final months, at not being there for her. Then the pause. As the importance of checking in is noted, dropping an email, a quick text. Small gestures. Big rescues.

*

An Anglican church near Elayn's flat will do for the service. The great fingers of Sydney Harbour on one side reach in to grab their lovely land, the ocean pounds sheer sandstone cliffs on the other. A little fist of a colonial church overlooks it all from its high vantage point, scoured by wind and sun. Water, water everywhere, and wind-toughened bush ringing the sandstone. Kookaburras and cockatoos, rosellas and bluetongue lizards among banksias and paperbarks, and a cram of ferns in the still clefts of rocks. Nature presses close. A faded ensign of old England hangs above the church's altar, stretching back to convict days – Elayn had two Second Fleeters in her family and was thrilled by that. It's all her. It's right.

*

The night before the funeral. Dressing the church hall for the wake, after adorning the church's pews with Elayn's scarves. With Andrew and my best friend, A, who has known my mother since she was ten. As we're coming clean to A about how Elayn actually died – the suicide, booze, pills – there's a splintering crash of thunder and a furious

156

burst of torrential rain, tropical and tetchy. We jump, laugh. Nervously. 'Yep, that's Elayn.'

She told me once that there was nothing beyond death and no, she wouldn't ever be looking down from heaven at the grandkids. Yet she feels present in spits of ferocious energy, goosebumps prick their way up our arms in a daddy-longlegs haunting. When Paul and I went back to her flat for some additional tidying up, her radio had somehow turned itself on and the electricity for her freezer had shorted, leaving us with a tub of spiteful rotting food. Shivery laughs as we got on with the clearing up, battening down into normality. But, but. Elayn, is that you? It sure feels like it.

*

The morning of the funeral, scrubbed and meek after the night's storm. A sullen, biblical sky. Standing room only. Numbers are difficult to estimate, we run out of memorial booklets. The funeral director, G, tells us Elayn has attracted an enormous number of single women, which is why we've been caught short. 'It's not like a funeral where there are a lot of families needing just one booklet between them. Your mum had a lot of friends. And most weren't attached to blokes.' A modelling shot is on the cover and many people are startled to see Elayn's beautiful auburn hair in her youth – she'd dyed her hair blonde from her twenties.

The music during the service is Gurrumul, the Aboriginal soprano from Arnhem Land with the achingly spiritual lament of a voice. Elayn loved his yearning, had his albums and a book of his life, had seen him live at the Opera House. Many of Elayn's friends have never heard of him. For a woman approaching old age she was effortlessly modern. Contemporary. Up to speed with the latest restaurants, plays, singers, and ways of death.

*

Elayn never felt old, in the way women a generation or two ago were little old ladies from their fifties onwards, faded into invisibility by the years. People in their seventies now dress like middle-aged people or younger; they drive, travel, they're on Facebook and vigorously socialise. It's a reason Elayn's death felt so shocking. She gave up. We weren't used to that.

*

Her funeral feels inclusive, funky, fun. I'm so tied up with making sure everything is just so that it passes in a blur of colour and singing and tributes; too fast. I want Mum to love it; want her to be proud of me for getting all the details right as a mark of my love for her; and it is right, it works beautifully. I'm so busy looking out for everyone else – guests not seen for decades, young children, elderly neighbours, old family friends, my father, a babysitter for toddlers – that I barely have time to cry. In fact, don't. I'm cried out, there's nothing left in me right now.

*

Elayn had been due for a casual shift at Parliament House the Tuesday following her death; a colleague speaks movingly. She concludes with a tribute from a Parliamentary sitting that had the State's politicians rising to their feet.

> The Speaker: 'It is with sadness that I report the passing of Elayn Gemmell, who was a valued casual member of the switchboard team for the past 13 years. Elayn passed away suddenly on 23 October 2015. Elayn was the mother of Mark, Paul and Nikki and known as Nonna by her much adored six grandchildren. She was a beautiful, fun-loving and gentle person. Elayn always approached her work with professionalism, dedication and enthusiasm and was extremely proud to work for the Parliament of New South Wales. She will be sorely missed by all who knew her.'

The colleague explained that members and officers of the House, the entire chamber, then stood in their places as a mark of respect for Elayn.

In the churchyard afterwards the grandchildren release balloons that match the riot of flowers on Elayn's smart white coffin, into a tall blue sky. G, the funeral director, and B, the vicar, walk slowly behind the hearse, side by side, as it's driven solemnly out the iron church gates by a woman in her broad-brimmed hat. It's a deeply moving image. The couple from the local restaurant, where we'd had Ticky's birthday dinner less than a fortnight before, do the catering for the wake. We offer up Elayn's favourite celebratory tipple, bubbles with orange and mango juice, her tropical Bellini. Elayn would have loved it. All of it. We got it right.

*

Yet Boh cannot stand up to do his poetry reading. He'd insisted on speaking at the funeral but broke down when he saw the confronting sight of the coffin at the altar. I hadn't prepared the children for that: Nonna dead in a box, with us yet not. My boy is a heave of weeping throughout the service. For months he's been the thirteen year old going through all the normal, clanging, hormonal changes, and now this. Various family members hold him; most fiercely, myself. Without a word Boh's older brother, Ticky, takes his poem and reads it for him when it's his turn and he cannot. With all this, the family is growing up.

Gleaning a truth here: of the imperative to be more tender with family members, only that. Everyone has their struggles. I looked across often at my fragile, broken Boh during those days, lost in a place I cannot completely reach. Know that I have to learn to give up the children to the wild places; the wild places that are not mine. Every parent does.

*

R – a friend of Elayn's in her eighties – grips my fist after the service, tighter than it's ever been held. 'You're now a part of the S.W.S.,' she whispers.

'What's that?'

'The Strong Women's Society.' She speaks as if this is a highly secret, select organisation to which I've suddenly, finally, been granted honorary membership. Mum was a member of it too, R declares; she had been for decades. Holding on to that. Seizing her interpretation of the unknowable; still, the unknowable.

*

At the service's conclusion, Boh breaks down once again. Stays in the church, embarrassed. His godmother, C, locks him in stillness. When everyone has left the church she brings him out to Andrew. Our boy is too distraught to let go of the balloons with the rest of the children. His father

161

takes him behind the church hall with a yellow one, his favourite colour. Boh stabs it and stabs it, with all the fury of a child whose grandmother has abandoned him.

*

In the five years we've been back from London we've been to a lot of funerals with the children. Uncles, a great-grandmother, old family friends and now this. It's anchored us here, to death as well as life; in England they never experienced them. Suburbs and streets, in several Australian cities, are now solemnly marked. Before this funeral we had Win's, Elayn's mother. She died peacefully in her nursing home in a pneumonia-triggered coma, with soft music and candles and strategically placed booklets about the changes the body undergoes as it enters the final stages, and slips away. But there was one funeral the children didn't go to – Lexi's, Bob's mother. Their other great-grandmother's.

She was 101. Had started sleeping a lot; a sign, I've learnt, that the end is near. Her funeral wishes were beautiful in their austerity but singular. Just her son and daughter were to be present as she was lowered into her husband's grave at Kurri Kurri in the Hunter Valley; her old stomping ground. No church, no priest. A bush taut with sound around her. Her children's loyal spouses were not to be present, nor any of her grandkids or great-grandkids; we were to remember her in our own way. Bob, as the new head of the family, was stubborn despite protests. 'The services aren't what they used to be, when they were big community events. It's what she wanted. And none of her friends are left.'

Elayn, so many decades younger, had plenty of friends left and most of them turned up. Twenty more years of life left in her and at her funeral, a lot of bewilderment.

*

Lexi was a sharp old thing: she knew what would work. There's something so sad about the funeral of an elderly person with pews pockmarked by emptiness. She didn't want the accusation of that. Lexi knew of the curse of elderly loneliness, a modern blight. As she was being lowered into her grave I was sitting on a jetty with a thermos of tea, her favourite tipple, and her beloved art deco teacup; remembering the old, broad, Hunter Valley vowels. The way she'd call a scourer a 'scratcher' and movies 'walkie-talkie photos'. The way she'd scorn a neighbour, 'As silly as a wet hen,' and hoot, 'It's snowing down south!' if my vintage petticoat was poking from under my skirt. As she was being lowered into the ground I remembered the bicarb soda she'd use to green the veggies up, the dishes never quite clean enough and the choko vine growing over the back fence. But most of all I remembered her lightness as the aging took hold of her, and the raucous laughter with it, as if

163

growing old was a process of becoming more light-hearted, and wondrous, at the beauty of so much around her. Lexi was all wonder towards the end. The opposite of Elayn.

*

Lexi had been specific: she was non-church going, didn't want an unknown priest. I've been to funerals where grief is compounded by anger at the seeming indifference of the religious figure before us, as if they're thinking more about the roast dinner ahead of them than the people around them. Anger, not only for the person who's died but for the church itself. Because it's a captive audience. Many in the congregation rarely go to church and it's a moment for the big sell. So, do it. Embrace the mystery of the institution you represent, win us over. We may have read our Richard Dawkins but we could, possibly, be partial to seduction.

*

What is loved: the family and friends who speak at a funeral, who distil a life to its essence of goodness. Rabbis often end a memorial service with 'May his memory be for a blessing' – meaning, what lesson can we learn from this person? A man I was in love with: To live vividly and with passion. A fellow school mum: The tonic of her joy. An old school mate: The gift of her friendship, the grace in her living. A near neighbour: The shine of him near the end, as if his last years were spent in a perpetual state of chuckle. So many aphorisms picked up during services and jotted on scrabbled receipts: Never suppress a kind thought. Be generous of spirit because it's bloody hard, for all of us. Pick up that phone. Check in. Love well.

Lexi loved well. 'People living deeply have no fear of death,' Anaïs Nin said, and Lexi had no fear about living deeply, no fear about doing things her way. It's the lesson I learnt from a life driven by love and laughter, the hoot of which I'll carry forever in my head. She wasn't bound by what other people thought of her – and with that, achieved an extraordinary lightness of being. And like choir boys reaching a heartbreakingly higher purity just as their voices are about to break, she became piercingly perceptive towards the end, telling us what's what. She sang 'My Way', loudly, delighting in its message. I wished I'd recorded her. Voice lodges longest in memory, can plunge us searingly back. I cannot bring myself to scrub Elayn's voice on my mobile messaging service. It's all I have of the sound of her, and it's a good, warm sound bite.

*

The funeral does not cauterise. My mind is still full, still churning. I catch myself talking to myself for days, weeks afterwards. Is this madness, a swamping, a great unhinging?

I lose my keys and wallet and my phone crashes and the world has been made awry, nothing is calm, nothing in its place. I am existing in a maelstrom of wrong and need to get on the other side of it. Need stillness. The cleanness of it. I'm still waking every 3 a.m.; oh for a good night's sleep, the sated sleep after sex. I fear my back cementing into a stoop, can feel the concrete clench of it even in slumber. Fear becoming preternaturally old through stress, through the body's uncanny mirroring of the parent via excessive trauma. I sleep on my back at night, trying to iron myself out. Who will unlock me now – if not myself?

*

Several weeks on, I collapse. At another funeral for another mother of a school friend. It's too soon after my mother's, too soon. I am hollowed out by grief. Can barely walk into the church. Am wound, just that. Have to leave halfway through. Everything is wrong. I am a peril to myself and to others. Need to be there for my friend but can't. Am knocked sideways by this new world. Boh and myself, Ticky and Paul, each of us struggling. All needing a cloistering from this.

*

Panic attacks, in the early hours. About so much ahead. So many years of parenthood to push through before I'm out, clear, on the other side. Before I'm allowed my life back. Sixty-four by the time my youngest leaves school; straight from motherhood into old age. Too old, too tired for this, a thirty-year stretch of active mothering; I did it wrong. I need a break from this life to get the energy to dive back into it. No pension arrangements, no superannuation since resigning from the ABC several decades ago and we will most likely have to sell our family home to fund our later years yet our children will still be young. That is our future. The price we paid, that the whole family will pay, for creative freedom during the adult years. Living the heart-in-mouth life of a freelancer with four children under sixteen. I have let my kids down with this scrabbling, creative, indulgent life. Four little people crowding into all corners of my existence, never needing me more and a hum of anxiety now staining all my days. No longer the energy for disrupting and never did enough of it anyway. Everything defeating me. In crisis. Mid-life crisis.

And Mum is now the finest of builder's dust. Everywhere. Cannot be clear of it. I have been the un-needing, the un-wanting, for all of my life but now, but now, I am vanquished. The funeral fixes nothing, just clears the people away. Ahead, a desert of grief to be crawled through. No end in sight.

167

17

Tilting full on now into what is feeling like madness. Becoming someone else entirely. Exploding with anger at close friends, severing relationships, plumped with tears. Elayn is infecting me, weakening me, could destroy me in the end. Now I know why the traditional period of mourning demands a necessary disappearing. It is to save you from yourself.

*

Favourite shoes vanish. No idea how. Where have I kicked them off? A café, a beach? The laptop slips off the bed while Jages is bouncing on it. It lands on the floor, an almighty thud. Everything lost of course. Because that is the way of the world now. The horror of a blank screen. No hard drive, no data. A month's worth of columns, including one on Elayn's death, plus a novel not saved. The Apple store cannot help. They give me the name of a spyware company that extracts data lost in flood and fires. No guarantees.

The damaged hard drive is sent to Brisbane. I wait. At great expense, everything is retrieved. And then, of course, the most distressing loss of the lot.

The ceramic lanterns. In a furious gust of wind from the Gods, sweeping through the house with its energy of disquiet.

*

I've never liked that Le Corbusier maxim, 'A house is a machine for living in.' For me it's more 'A house is a mooring for living in.' A necessary sanctuary of stillness amid the great gallop of life; a place that loosens you as you step across the threshold; releasing you into a space where you can relax into your true self. This house is my lair, now, as I crack.

*

And now, now, the line of porcelain lanterns. The final straw. The lanterns that have spread their calm over every living area of whatever house we're in, in whatever country. They feel like love itself, childhood and memory. All the history of the children's growing up in their scratches and pin pricks. Gone.

*

To remember: the concept of *Kintsugi*. The quiet salve of it. An accepting of the old and imperfect, the forgiveably human. Years ago, Elayn and I had holidayed in Japan then Cuba. We'd slept in the same bed in the tiniest of Tokyo hotel rooms, always at our best when travelling, slipping together like hand into glove. Had the same food habits and bedtimes, the same love of shopping. When we were good we were very, very good …

In Japan, we were introduced to *Kintsugi*. Marvelled at healed cracks with their threads of repairing gold. The practice first arose when a shogun, Ashikaga Yoshimasa, accidently smashed a favoured tea bowl. He sent it to China for repair and was horrified by the crude fix that returned. The careless ugliness. In anger, Yoshimasa commanded his own craftsmen to devise a different means of repair. They came up with a technique involving resin and gold powder, which gave the shattered, cherished object a new watertight strength.

With the Apollonian concepts of symmetry and perfection there's the absence of messy, warm, irrepressible life. With *Kintsugi*, the repaired object bears the scars of existence and is made even more striking because we can suddenly relate; an all too human story, from an all too human hand.

*

In Japan, some ceramic objects are broken on purpose so they can be mended using the *Kintsugi* method. The lacquer takes on the form of waterfalls, cascades, drips. The result, a startling new look. More intriguing than the bloodless, bland original.

*

The love demonstrated in the *Kintsugi* object should encourage us to respect what is damaged; find beauty in it. That should begin with our parents. I never saw beauty enough, with Elayn. Others did. I never let her know I saw her beauty. I did not love her well enough. Do those whose sharp edges have been softened by sorrow love better? I will love better now. More empathetically.

*

Standing, frozen, at the top of the stairs. Staring at the lanterns shattered beyond repair. Rushing to the bin as Andrew is about to tip the jagged pieces into it. Gathering them up, spilling them onto the dining table. Keening at all the tiny, slivery bits, so many, too many, that don't seem to fit anywhere. Impossible, everything impossible. 'Keep them,' Andrew says.

*

Elayn would throw out any piece of broken crockery. Discard it at the slightest chip. She said germs nestled in the crevices. She loved the new, the smart, the dazzling. Everything was about public image and perfection. She couldn't bear the almost-solid matter in a cracked egg – the gelatinous sliver of an embryo – and would meticulously pick it out; everything had to be right. I did not fit into her carefully curated world. I was awkward, shy, stroppy. Loved my uni-black and vintage tat and my ugly Blundstone boots. When I lived in the Northern Territory, as an ABC radio correspondent, Elayn would say, 'When are you going into television?' Alert me to ads in the Sydney TV newsrooms. Interpret my lack of interest in television as a fatal flaw that signified a lack of drive. Saw radio journalism as a stepping stone to the glories of the small screen; whereas I saw radio journalism as a stepping stone into writing.

Elayn flung at me once that my living in Alice Springs was about being 'unable to cope'. She had no idea that it was a place of expansive uncurling. I felt alive there, within the desert hum. In Sydney I felt judged, hemmed in, reduced. I always needed to put a little distance between myself and the world. And always there were Elayn's admonishments to step out into that world, get my head out of a book and stop hiding behind glasses. 'Me' wasn't what she wanted. In Alice Springs, I felt the potential of release.

She had so many opinions about my life. About how I looked, who I went out with, what job I took. I've always walked a singular path into happiness – it was not my mother's idea of happiness. So, the flinty alone. The desert hum. The Holden ute. Clothes she did not understand I needed to wear, life choices she did not understand I needed to make.

*

I've not spoken to Mum for many weeks, since I told her I was thinking of moving to the desert. And she told me she wants a Jana Wendt daughter. We hung up. I am lost, mother. This has to be done, this move. I've half of a first draft of a novel in the computer. I have to see. Just have to.
Journal entry, mid-twenties.

*

Elayn's fear of being stained by who I'd become. To me I was strong with my own voice; to her, I was unmouldable. She didn't speak to her own mother for months, years, after Win wore a tracksuit to a family wedding. My grandmother was in her nineties and wanted comfort; Elayn was mortified. 'It's an embarrassing fact,' philosopher Susan Neiman wrote in her book *Why Grow Up*, 'that we are often more afraid of embarrassment than a host of other discomforts, but it isn't less true for that.' So much of Elayn's existence

173

was tethered to public image. She couldn't control all the strong women in her life. Win. Me.

*

'Is it possible to succeed without any act of betrayal?' Jean Renoir asked. With Elayn, I was always writing myself into a different narrative, far away from her world. I never expected our intertwined story to take the path it has now, to converge so traumatically. I thought I was free of her. I'm not good at walking this new path.

*

Five years ago I came home. The place the poet Les Murray said you return to to go mad.

Five years ago I felt rescued by a looser, lighter life. Freshly returned to Australia after fifteen years away, to a little seaside pocket with kookaburras on the Hills Hoist and neighbourhood kids zooming through houses; to the whole blissful Aussie childhood I thought long lost. My pale little Londoners slipped into this new world like dirty mugs into a dishwasher. We gazed up at the stretched glory of the starry night then they'd tumble into bed exhausted from running about in all the sunshine – that was growing them tall, that was honey-ing them up. And I ruminated on why it had taken us so long to come back. London had stolen my optimism. Australia restored it. I felt like I was being immersed in a sense of belonging, something I fought tooth and nail against in the younger, wilder years. But I needed it as I aged. Had never had it in London no matter how long we were there.

Returning was about the serenity and stillness that comes from being part of a deeply known world; the *ease* of it. Andrew and I had spent years being outsiders in foreign lands and revelling in that status; but my God, the relief, suddenly, of belonging. After so long. Of existing in a familiar world. It was hitting us like a long cool drink after a sweltering summer's day. I celebrated the solace of familiarity; the thrumming, throat-swelling joy at being home. England, stimulating, yes – but my heart was held hostage by the Great Southern Land and the yearning had only increased as the years gathered pace.

In exile I learnt one thing above all: that life is about wringing the most happiness we can out of our time on earth, and for me that meant family. And beauty – a muscular Australian beauty, not the soft, benign European one. Under a replenishing sun. I was a plant turning towards the light, drinking it up. I'd finally found my place in the world and was blazing contentment and revelling in the gift of belonging, and growing up. It was called home.

*

But now, severed from that sense of home. 'I am always conscious of this secret disruption in me,' Katherine Mansfield wrote. I feel as if my entire discourse with Elayn, from fifteen onwards, involved a secret disruption. Or perhaps not so secret. Perhaps she sensed it all along and could not control it. Which enraged her.

Eyes come at me, into me, wherever I go now. I'm treading warily into the wider world, at odds with it, trembling and stunned and stopped. Like that small animal frozen in headlights, still, weeks and months beyond the morgue shock. The world of my growing up, that I ran away from aged thirty, is now rubbing up too close; judging, questioning, assessing. And I have failed at this great homecoming experiment. My lanterns are broken and so am I. No energy to fix them, no energy for anything. Shardy and wrong. What is needed: an armoury for living. And binocular eyes to see far into the future. To see if all this can be climbed away from.

18

A call out of the blue from Constable B.

Several months beyond Mum's death. We'd assumed that the entwined worlds of the police and ourselves were long over. But no. The wheels turn slowly with investigations like this. Constable B needs me to come to the police station for a statement about Elayn. I've never done such a thing before.

Harrowing me back to those fraught, early days of Elayn's death.

*

Was it an accident? The churn of the old question afresh. Head cram, all over again. Elayn had no makeup, no lipstick and was wearing old clothes at the time of death yet made a will and organised an alcohol delivery just before she died. All the conflicting signals. Calm has gone astray, all over again.

*

Constable B is from somewhere similar to where Elayn escaped from. It is in her voice, her rising inflections, the way she says 'youse' instead of 'you'. In the way she needs her grammar corrected as she types up my statement and is grateful for it, as we sit side by side, trying to work this out. She is keen to know Mum's drug past, in stark detail. She will be investigating Elayn's doctor – doctors – and her medical history. She needs to know if there's been negligence by anyone who dealt with Elayn.

I have to tell her everything I know. It runs to several pages over several hours. It is a Friday night. Constable B assures me she has the time, 'Outside hasn't hotted up yet.' I can't tell her much about Elayn's doctor shopping. I don't know, and am ashamed of this. Except I do know that Elayn was high on drugs after the foot operation and it evened her, there was a quietening. Within her, and with her relationships. Drugs = a good thing when it came to Elayn. For a while. With all the rest, the details, I didn't examine the situation closely enough. Constable B's questions are an indictment.

All the torment, back. Just when I'm possibly finding a way out of it.

*

Constable B wants to know about the missing $2,000. That Elayn withdrew on my watch, several days before her death. It's a mystery. I'm a cliché of adult-caregiver to a parent in the Western world: too busy, too caught up in my own life, drowning, not doing anything quite right. Constable B remarks that there are a lot of people on her beat in similar circumstances to my own.

I tell her that when my brothers and I went into the flat for another clean-up we found vials of a mysterious clear liquid, with a pinkish tinge, in plastic tubes in Elayn's freezer. We had no idea what it was. We threw it out. Didn't think to retain it as evidence. Of what? Could it have been Nembutal, the illegal animal tranquilliser, which is sometimes stained pink for safety reasons? We don't know. Constable B shrugs.

*

Her job is distressing at times. 'I get emotional. I had to leave twice as you were identifying your mother.' I had no idea of this at the time. 'No one knows that side of the job, how hard it can be,' she adds. Constable B says that Elayn's actions are surprisingly common in this leafy, middle-class area. 'No one talks about it.' She says there was one difference between my mother's death and the many other suicide situations involving elderly people that she's attended. 'They were all suffering from depression.' I tell

her that Elayn possibly had undiagnosed depression. That it
had blighted her life. Constable B nods. Types.

*

This is the last of it for me, for the official situation.
Constable B now has a lot of digging to do. As I depart I
ask her again if she thinks it was deliberate. With infinite
sadness in her eyes this woman in her mid-twenties – who's
seen all manner of life, too young – nods. 'Yes.' Later, at
home, I feel like I've run a marathon. I fall into bed,
drained.

*

And then, and then. The day after I give the police
statement Ticky goes through the glass doors at the back
of the house. Four fifteen-year-old boys are at home with
the younger kids while Andrew is overseas and I'm around
the corner at a dinner party. Two of the teenage lads are
mucking about, one pushing a glass door one way, one
the other. The glass breaks, of course it breaks. Boh calls,
barely able to push talk out, in a voice I've never heard
from him before. 'Blood. E-e-everywhere.' A call no parent
wants to get.

*

Running around the corner, blind, having grabbed someone else's glasses from the dinner table. But I can see well enough to discern my eldest covered in blood from neck to ankles as I race into the house. His right arm is ribboned. A glass fragment has sliced through his neck. An ex-doctor neighbour, also at the dinner party, runs in right behind me. Sits my boy down, clamps his fingers to his neck, feels a pulse. Oh God, oh God, too much of everything here. The man turns to me. Tells me he will live but he needs stitches. Tells me later that the cut was an inch from the carotid artery and if it had been severed my son would have bled out in ten minutes and there would have been nothing he could have done to save him.

Please. Relief. From this year. This life.

*

So. The inner workings of an ambulance now, straight after the inner workings of a police station. Stroking my boy's head. He's covered in blood and Snapchatting and Instagramming his war wounds and tallying the likes. Of course. A social media opportunity. The printed sign at the foot of the stretcher, for every patient to note: 'Please treat your ambulance officer like you would your grandmother.' They don't say 'mother', of course. That one doesn't work anymore, the emotional resonance is no longer as tugging. But 'grandmother', well, that's different.

*

'Have you been drinking?' The first question from the A & E doctor when she clocks the fact that four fifteen-year-old lads have been larking about. Ticky hasn't, hasn't begun with that world, but I can feel pressures closing in on me here from all sides, like a diver fighting the weight of deep, cold water. Need now to end.

*

Who knows? That you are cracking apart but soldiering on but not. Breakdown is voluminously lonely, and silent. One friend, J, notices. She has been through extreme grief and recognises it; she says I am like a car running on empty with a hole in its fuel tank, faulty, and unable to run right. She urges me to see a counsellor. It feels like failure. Too busy, no time. She says most women around me would have seen a therapist at some stage. Brain pain. Thought pain. Perhaps she's right.

19

A letter from the coroner eventually arrives. 'Following consideration of relevant advice from police officers and medical practitioners, and other appropriate persons, the Coroner is satisfied that the date, place, manner and cause of the death of Elayn GEMMELL have been sufficiently disclosed. Consequently, the coroner has dispensed with the holding of an inquest. The cause of death has been established as: Multi Drug Toxicity.'

Three words. The answer to everything, and not even specific. Officially the case is closed. There will be no hearing, no one put under the spotlight. A story all too common in this day and age. What is needed: the lushness of absolutely knowing. A blanket of understanding to crawl under and sleep, finally sleep. To put it all to rest. Why? Endlessly the question, why?

*

In Elayn's final week she was trapped in her flat, relying on a busy daughter and sons who lived several hours away as well as a small network of available friends, not many. She hated calling on any of us. Hated expressing need. Public transport was available but difficult, irregular and slow. From this point, it must have felt there was no way back into life.

*

Savage pain in her final months was affecting Elayn's sleeping, moving, walking. It was hard for her to find a comfortable seat. The right bed. To shower for a long amount of time. It affected how she dressed – certain clothes became more difficult to put on and fashionable shoes impossible to wear. The shock, when searching for funeral clothes, to find the blunt, squat, rubber-soled shoes lined up like obedient schoolgirls; rows of drabness after a lifetime of fabulous foot glory. This is what fashion had done to my audacious mother; reduced her to this meekness; row upon hoarded row of it. All worn for nothing but comfort in the final years of her life.

*

With chronic pain, one of the most distressing things to relinquish can be care over dressing. Pain puts wrinkles on your face because of the tight set of your muscles. Affects your posture and teeth, brittles and breaks them. A bra becomes difficult to navigate, and underpants, and the zip up your back. You lose the ability to present your best self to the world. For Elayn, who had spent her life being noticed, this was all, utterly, devastating. Her final clothes in the morgue shout of the decline – the faded tracksuit pants, the ratty old t-shirt. Elayn was so rarely this. Pain had caused her to become someone else. Who she hated.

*

In her final weeks Elayn asked me to investigate physiotherapists who could come to her flat and help her. I sent her an email with links.

> Big thank you for the info Nikki. I have opened the first
> one and it looks wonderful. However, I'm feeling too frail
> to follow up just now, just need to rest my body.

In hindsight, she'd given up. And despite all the doctors and specialists she was seeing, all the morphine patches and pills, her pain was inadequately managed. It's a brutal truth.

*

186

The final doctor Elayn saw, an Indian man, was different. 'I know what you're doing with all your doctors. And if you don't stop I'll report you.' Paul told me this; that Elayn had finally been found out. The system was onto her – her steady supply of painkillers would be reduced. The panic, the fear.

*

The first thing you do, as an addict, is start lying. My mother had lost her identity to that of a drug addict. You have to lie to doctors to get drugs. It involves shame. That was Elayn's world towards the end. Dishonesty, fudging, pretending. How must it feel that you need drugs so much you're lying to a doctor? And not just one, but several. In your seventies, after a lifetime of fine, upstanding living, when you've never been to a police station before. The loneliness of it. The humiliation.

*

Researchers have discovered that morphine can actually make chronic pain worse. Writing in the *Proceedings of the National Academy of Sciences*, they concluded that rats given morphine were more sensitive to pain than those not given it. Rats on the drug took longer to recover, and it was accompanied by more severe pain. Elayn said the

187

pain was getting worse six months beyond her operation; was spreading, taking over her life. Report co-author, neuroscientist Dr Peter Grace: 'The treatment can actually be contributing to the problem.' Well yes.

*

Addiction is not a liberation but a prison. It generates self-loathing. The pattern: short periods of release followed by long periods of despair. Self-hatred and secrecy are cleaved to it. Many of Elayn's closest friends had no idea of her drug habit, of how she was getting through life.

*

With chronic pain, you become intolerant to the drugs. You can develop a different pain in a different area of your body. It has a domino effect. A foot problem causes a knee problem then a hip problem then a back problem. Elayn wouldn't let me in, wouldn't discuss pain management, in a pattern that had marked her life. We should have had the conversation.

*

Elayn wasn't always a truthful person with me. I bought her a car more than a decade ago with book royalties; years later she denied this had ever happened despite the transfer to the car company appearing on my bank statement. 'No you didn't!' she spat in my face at the height of some rage, point-blank denying it. It was in those moments I thought Elayn mad. My father told me he had sent her to a psychiatrist during their divorce; her mother spoke of her mental instability. We'd all experienced the bluntness of inconsistency; most of her friends, though, hadn't. It's hard to have a solid relationship with someone who's not truthful, especially when it's a family member. Dishonesty is a key to destroying any relationship.

*

Elayn was fascinating because she wasn't quite right. It made her intriguing, glamorous. She was her own version of *Kintsugi*; her flaws added to the charisma. She was enigmatic, captivating, a little dangerous; and until the bleak final months all eyes around her had always been on her.

Elayn's non-married state gave her an edge because she was truly free. It was what she wanted. Free of a partner, and in the end free of her children. She wanted the comforting alone, where no one would judge. Elayn had mastered the art of the exquisitely damaging retreat.

*

Seeing a counsellor feels like weakness, embarrassment, as if there is some mental deficiency; I know this is ridiculous. I visit my GP and get a name, don't want anyone I know. Steel myself. V has a leonine grey bob on a young face. Her only concession to beauty is a slash of red lipstick. She seems fearless.

It is balming. She is on my side. V tells me I must not let this define me, must not let this destroy me. She is on Elayn's side too. She says that suicide is sometimes a distorted altruism; not seen by the person who does it as a selfishness, but a selflessness. They can feel, misguidedly, that the world would be better off without them. I think of all the people I've known, the too-many people, who've taken their life. Most through a distorted sense of goodness. That this was the right thing to do for them, and for everyone else.

Oh Mum.

V tells me she spoke to a healer once, in her younger days, who said to think of the lost person with love, just that. Yes.

*

Depression is often anger turned in on itself. Elayn couldn't articulate what her fury was about but she could show it; and with her most spectacular act of all, her death. This was payback, suggests V. 'There was probably an underlying, undiagnosed depression there too.'

*

Boh finds the letter from the coroner. Reads the bald summary. 'Cause of Death: Multi Drug Toxicity.' Knows what that means because he's sat through many personal development classes at school about drugs. The curt, official words sound shameful, reducing; a junkie's world. Yet my son's expensively groomed, cultured grandmother came across as anything but that. His face crumples. 'So … Nonna committed suicide?' He, like me, had been hoping it was some terrible mistake. The letter seems to refute this. Back into his shell of grief.

*

Multi Drug Toxicity means an overdose from different types of pills. Dependency and addiction are different things. Dependency means you are dependent on drugs; addiction means you crave them. My mother, in the end, was an addict. Her drug of choice, oxycodone, has another name: Hillbilly Heroin. It was a squalid, junkie's death.

My poor, reduced, despairing, alone mother.

20

Elayn could be the poster girl for this Era of Pain Mismanagement.

Opioid addiction is the US's worst drug crisis in decades. In the UK, reasearchers from Imperial College London claim almost half the adult population is living with chronic pain, and their major problem is a lack of effective treatment. In Australia, the issue is also problematic. It is vining our aging world. On one side, doctors on the frontline of pain alleviation and on the other, drug industry groups. The reality: the drugs don't work well enough.

*

What no expert refutes: opioid drugs are highly addictive. As Elayn discovered. And sometimes, despairingly, pain is a cul-de-sac – there's no way out of it, no way to relieve it. In 2016 the US government finally took action over opioid abuse after years of controversy, publishing the first national standards for prescription painkillers. The new

US guidelines are nonbinding but it's hoped they'll create a river of change in current medical practice. Dr Andrew Kolodny, the head of Physicians for Responsible Opioid Prescribing, describes the US standards as one of the most significant medical interventions ever, by government: 'This is the first time the federal government is communicating clearly to the medical community that the risks outweigh the potential benefits of these drugs.'

Their recommendations:

- Doctors first try ibuprofen and aspirin to treat pain.
- Opioid treatment for short-term pain lasts for three days maximum and rarely more than seven.
- Patients have their urine tested before getting prescriptions.
- Doctors check prescription drug tracking systems to ensure patients aren't doctor shopping.

All these measures combined would have prevented Elayn's slippery slope to oblivion.

*

At the heart of the epidemic is a drug industry wanting to maximise profits. At the heart of the epidemic is no national, real-time system of prescription monitoring; it's too easy to doctor shop. At the heart of the epidemic are doctors who don't speak loudly enough of the risks of opioids when prescribing them. Doctors who hit the print button and have no time to explain, because the next person is already in the busy waiting room and the next. They need to talk things through, detail potential problems.

*

The US government's recommendations are a major about-turn from the giddy days of the nineties, which saw a rapid explosion of opioid use after claims they could be used for back pain and arthritis without fear of addiction. This was untrue. Before this, doctors had been accused of under-treating pain. But as opioid use rapidly increased, so did overdoses. And deaths.

*

Doctors were once told that opioids like OxyContin or oxycodone were safe – and now they're being told the opposite. All too late for Elayn. As a medical condition, pain is difficult to measure. The ability to tolerate it, or not, is highly individual. In my mother's case a doctor wrote a short-term prescription for opioid use which triggered a long-term reliance. Did they have any idea what they were getting Elayn into? It seems that they did not – or did not care.

*

It's estimated that one in five Australians suffers chronic pain, which is classified as severe pain lingering beyond three months. There are different types and different options for treatment. Use of painkillers is only one. Elayn didn't know enough about alternatives. I believe she would always have euthanised herself, just not at this point if she had investigated proper pain management. I wish she had considered a pain clinic, a specialist multi-disciplinary alternative. In Australia they're underfunded, under-resourced and not well known enough.

*

Researchers from the International Narcotics Control Board reported on the use of opioid painkillers – such as codeine, morphine and oxycodone – for most countries between 2001–03 and 2011–13. The researchers found that the worldwide use doubled across the period, and in Australia, more than quadrupled. Professor Richard Mattick, of the National Drug and Alcohol Research Centre, says patients may be staying on drugs too long – which increases tolerance, and makes the pills ineffective.

*

The drug industry and some pain doctors bitterly oppose opioid guidelines. They argue new rules will create unfair hurdles for some patients.

There have been heartening strides in the treatment of cancer and heart disease over the past decades, yet relatively few when it comes to the epidemic of chronic joint pain. The situation's becoming worse as our population ages. What also needs a lot more research: the correlation between chronic pain and depression. People with persistent pain often have a pull towards depression, as the pain is traumatising all aspects of their life, not just the injured area. It can wear you down, deplete your energy, flatten you. But which comes first? Chronic pain can be magnified by depression; depression can be magnified by chronic pain. They share the same nerve pathways as well as neurotransmitters – brain chemicals acting as messengers between the nerves. It's a vicious cycle.

A combustible combination: the person prone to depression suddenly catapulted into the world of sustained pain. That was Elayn. Pain was her bully, constantly nibbling away at her equilibrium.

*

What are also linked: pain and social isolation. It's easy to burrow into your own tight little world in the thick of the pain, too easy. So few of us knew of the cruelty of Elayn's new master.

Codeine is the elephant in the room. Products containing it are restricted in some countries, but in Australia they're still available over-the-counter at chemists. Some experts have proposed that people should have a doctor's script to buy painkillers like Nurofen Plus and Panadeine, as well as flu medicines containing codeine. It caused an outcry at the time, yet the experts were concerned about 'medical misadventure' through codeine abuse. Fatal overdoses more than doubled between 2000 and 2009. The contentious proposal followed the release of a national policy framework, which warned that painkillers and tranquillisers were causing increasing addiction and overdoses. With our aging population there's concern that painful conditions and anxiety disorders are on the rise – which means a new, older generation of drug addicts. Like Elayn.

*

The organisation Pain Australia has issued guidelines for heading into the great battle with chronic pain. It urges a thorough understanding of the medicines being administered. But the organisation believes that drugs alone aren't the answer. It labels medicine as 'passive therapy', and wants sufferers to be actively involved in managing their pain. This includes daily stretching and walking, factoring in rest and stretch breaks, and practising relaxation techniques like yoga – because when muscles are tightened they increase pressure on nerves and tissues, which maximises pain. And it encourages sufferers to find support, because chronic pain can be an incredibly isolating experience. No one understands.

Elayn was shockingly isolated. I didn't realise how lonely pain can make you, or how profoundly it can transform a life. There was the euphoric joy after her foot operation: 'I'm as high as a kite!' There were months of the best time of our adult lives. 'Look at my morphine patch, Nik, isn't it pretty?' But then the turning, the rapid turning, that drove her to her death.

*

Doctors are now being offered training about opioids and chronic pain, and being urged to consider other remedies. Physical therapy, acupuncture, antidepressants, counselling. But alternatives are unrealistic for some people, or just not wanted. Elayn said she was too tired to investigate physiotherapy in her home. She tried acupuncture but it only gave limited relief, and she didn't have the energy for much else. In the end she just wanted her opioids. It's a highly stigmatised world. It is Elayn's truth. A lot of elderly people's truth.

21

For five years leading up to her death Elayn had been emailing the Australian euthanasia enabler Dr Philip Nitschke, and people in his organisation, Exit International. Philip tweeted about Elayn following the newspaper column I wrote, in anguish, asking if her death was empowerment or despair.

> Nikki, it was empowerment! – your mother joined,
> #euthanasia PP Handbook, asked Exit forum Qs and
> imported.

In his in-house euthanasia shorthand, Dr Nitschke was explaining that my mother had purchased his *Peaceful Pill Handbook*, attended his Exit forums, and imported the illegal drug Nembutal, which was indeed the mysterious pink liquid in her freezer. In other words, she had broken the law. With that knowledge, I felt like I was stepping into a parallel universe. Elayn? Really? How did she become this? I felt so much anger, shortly after her death, at this euthanasia industry. At Dr Nitschke's tweet about my mother, at the business of empowered death. Anger that his world makes it too easy and too private if you want that. That it enables people like Elayn to do it their way, all by themselves. Without pesky family or friends.

*

Nembutal is sometimes sent by importers in perfume bottles to escape Customs detection. In Australia the drug is sent from Mexico, sometimes China. It's a barbiturate used by vets to put animals down, known as 'Green Dream', and was once prescribed as a sleeping pill for humans. As a family, we don't know who Elayn got to help her with delivery as it's highly risky to get it sent to your house. The Australian Government lists barbiturates as a border-controlled drug and states that their illegal importation may attract criminal sanctions. Penalties range from imprisonment and fines of up to $825,000. It's a lot to risk.

*

Dr Nitschke is a former physician. His book, *The Peaceful Pill Handbook*, details how to die with dignity by your own hand. A peaceful, reliable method of extinguishing life is, of course, what a lot of elderly people dream of. To die in our sleep, without struggle or trauma, unreliability, mess.

Knowledge is empowering. For a lot of older people, anxiety about end of life choices revolves around a lack of control. Ignorance tips into angst. Dr Nitschke's book argues that providing information does not encourage people to die by their own hand – it empowers them, which reduces anxiety. The *Handbook* explains that if an opiate like morphine, heroin or codeine is used it's likely to be peaceful. Morpheus, after all, was the Greek god of dreams and sleep.

In Western countries where assisted suicide is a crime – which is most – it's extremely difficult to work out how to kill yourself peacefully. And how to protect your family in the process. Elayn had done her research.

*

The penalties for helping someone to die are severe. In Australia, imprisonment ranges from five years to life. In the UK, it's up to fourteen years. Penalties in the US vary from state to state and only Oregon, Washington and Vermont allow assisted suicide, by a doctor. But strict residency rules apply. Nembutal is the drug of choice in all jurisdictions that allow it: Switzerland, the Netherlands, Belgium, and the handful of US states.

*

Philip Nitschke's organisation argues that assisted suicide should not necessarily be a medical event – you should be able to do it at home if you want to. The *Handbook* tallies up the effectiveness of various suicide methods, giving percentages for efficacy, peacefulness and reliability. Nembutal comes out on top. Overnight is advised as the optimal time for killing yourself, when others are asleep and it may be some time before you're discovered, which negates the risk of being found too soon – and revived.

The Peaceful Pill Handbook advises taking alcohol alongside any pills to trigger death, to nullify the bitter aftertaste and to expedite the extinguishing of life – commonly used lethal drugs work faster alongside it. One of the drinks recommended as an enabler is Baileys Irish Cream.

Elayn did it by the book.

*

Philip Nitschke claims he was the first doctor in the world to administer a voluntary and legalised lethal injection, when the practice was briefly allowed in Australia's Northern Territory in the mid-nineties. He facilitated the deaths of four people. 'It seems we demand humans to live with indignity, pain and anguish whereas we are kinder to our pets when their suffering becomes too much,' he explained at the time. 'It simply is not logical or mature. Trouble is, we have had too many centuries of religious claptrap.' A 'mature' approach. Elayn would have appreciated that. She liked to consider herself evolved.

Dr Nitschke works mainly with older people and is inspired by them – he says they see this way as a practical approach. He argues that an individual person has a fundamental right to control their own death, just as they have a right to control their own life. He believes in having a 'peaceful pill' available for every adult of sound mind, and questions the view that suicide in our modern times is always linked to depression and mental illness. His book details dying in a way that quarantines a person's family and friends from the scrutiny of the law.

*

Nitschke's *Handbook* advises that with Nembutal, sleep usually occurs within minutes of taking the drug alongside alcohol, and death within the hour. In the end Elayn chose not to use this method, despite managing to import it from Mexico from a supplier known to Dr Nitschke. Was she afraid that her batch had been contaminated; that it wasn't 'pure'? There have been concerns raised by euthanasia supporters in the past. There are testing kits for purity if you want to go down that path. Elayn was a thinker. In the end she opted to do it her way. She must have thought it was the best way to die. The most protective way. Of herself, and of others.

*

An elderly woman's voice was dismissed. By her family, by the wider world. But they listened at Exit. I track Philip down after his tweet. 'She [Elayn] was always a person who was very clear in her ideas,' he emails, 'and we were always pleased she was an Exit member.'

*

But I need to talk to him, need clues. He is open, sympathetic, considered. 'There was a lot of contact with us in the last six months as Elayn was negotiating the practicalities of giving herself this final choice,' he says on the phone. 'It's not uncommon for people like her to want to have their questions answered. But whether they want to talk with their families varies hugely. What you found is actually very common. Often people say to us, "Well, I haven't told my family." And when we ask why, one of the commonest remarks is that they're worried about any legal risk to family members. They don't want them to have any possibility of being caught up in the legal scenario. But another issue is that close family members will try and talk them out of it, or frustrate their plans. We've seen cases where children – thinking they're acting in the best interests – do things like steal the drugs, or involve the police or psychiatrists. We've seen the whole spectrum of views. And in some ways the Right to Die movement is sometimes responsible for building up a fear; that people feel they have to be alone. In some ways it's easier if the big discussions just don't occur. But the situation that works out best for everyone is when people are able to talk things through, and an understanding is reached. So that when the death takes place the children are left with positive memories.'

Philip says Elayn was troubled by the thought of involving overseas dealers in supplying her Nembutal. 'There are very predatory actions by the Australian authorities with attempts to intercept the importation of these drugs. Generally speaking, Australia has got a notorious reputation. That would have led to concern from Elayn about possible legal action for the receiver – in the case of assisting a suicide, you'd be looking at potentially fourteen years in jail, so all those things would have weighed on her mind.'

There's also concern among Exit members that they won't receive the right thing; that they might be cheated by an overseas dealer. 'People really want to know that something is going to work. They don't want to be messed around with something that might be salty or cut

205

in some way, so the question of testing comes up. In the last year or two, people have been very keen to test. That issue about not being too sure, that you might be getting caught up in some kind of fraud, may have weighed on her mind. From her phone message she sounded like a person who was very anxious to get reassurances about things.'

Of course she was. Elayn wanted effectiveness. The perfectionist would not have left anything to chance.

*

She got one of her doctors to contact Dr Nitschke, explaining her situation.

'That's a bit unusual, having a doctor write to us giving an outline of her situation. I'm quite surprised that he did it. He must have been reasonable. The medical records that she sent us are quite extensive. The letter is addressed to me; it says "I'm Elayn's treating doctor. She has asked me to explain to you that she's been suffering chronic pain due to various medical admissions over the last year, and these pains have not been responding to medical management or analgesics. We are trying to find the root cause but it has meant her mobility has been extremely poor for much of this time." She must have asked for that letter to be sent. I don't know why. And what is interesting is that as a doctor, he responded to that.'

Dr Nitschke adds, 'I'm sad Elayn had anxieties and concerns and a difficulty in getting information in the final months. She was fearful about who she talked to. It would have been so much better had she been more open about it. But she wanted to be careful, and wanted to protect people. But in the end I'm very pleased that she was able to put things together herself in a way that was exactly what she wanted.'

*

I ask Dr Nitschke about fears that the legalisation of euthanasia could lead to unscrupulous people pushing their elderly family members into deaths before the time of their own choosing.

'This is a common issue raised by those opposing change,' Dr Nitschke responds, 'that the vulnerable elderly will be pressured by unscrupulous relatives, and others, into doing the right thing etc. My response is that we currently see the elderly being pressured by family members; pressured to "keep fighting", often against some hopeless medical situation. I've had many, many elderly Exit members tell me that they're being urged by relatives to "not give up", to try this new drug/chemo/treatment, when all they want to do is to be allowed to peacefully die. This is the commonest reason given for why family members are not told of their involvement with Exit, or their decision to import – for fear their plans may be frustrated. So, this "pressure to die", if it were to occur were legislation to change, may balance the tyranny of the "pressure to live", which is currently sanctioned. The other observation is that the ready acceptance that this behaviour *will* occur is to assume that the elderly are, by their nature vulnerable, which is intrinsically ageist. I get annoyed by those who often raise these spectres as reasons why the status quo should be allowed to persist, while failing to acknowledge the totally unsatisfactory nature of the current situation.'

*

There is an ideological split that increasingly divides the euthanasia movement. As Dr Nitschke explains, it's 'between those who want control (over their death) and see it as paramount, their right; and those who seem happier to leave the decision making to the medical profession. I suspect Elayn was a believer in the former.'

*

How dare he, I had thought, in the days after Dr Nitschke's opportunistic tweet; assuming he was a craven peddler of death, just using my mother's tragedy to advertise his wares. But I know now that there's much more to the man than that. He is a humanitarian. He cares, deeply. Put simply, he wants to put people out of their misery in the most humane way possible. Elayn deeply respected that.

*

Dr Nitschke is now based in Switzerland and the Netherlands. 'Life became very difficult in Australia. The whole issue has become depressing. You can get weighed down by the ongoing struggles – there's a more enlightened environment over here. The debate in these parts is about whether everyone over a certain age should have access to these drugs. It's easier to work in the area over here. It upsets me a bit that we led the world briefly. In some ways, amazingly, the Northern Territory was a very progressive place, and now we've gone back into the dark ages. My own views have evolved. A person's ability to control their own death is a human right, rather than some conferred medical privilege. It's the philosophical debate taking place right now. There's been an evolution in thinking. The laws will pass.'

I began with him in anger, I end with him in respect.

*

The religious lobby is vehemently opposed to euthanasia, to the taking of a life in any way; it is God's choice and God's alone. Elayn's views on religion were final. Elayn didn't believe in God. When she said she would one day euthanise herself, and I had admonished her for not wanting to see the grandkids grow up, she'd batted her hands as if it was a minor consideration compared to the pain she was facing. There was no light. She surrounded herself with a boundary of no.

*

Elayn had several Catholic priests in her family in Western Australia and sent us to Sunday school as children. Yet gradually she withdrew from the churchiness so deeply embedded in her suburban world of the sixties and seventies. We'll never know why she had the number for the Victims of Child Abuse in her address book, never know if there's a connection between that, and her Catholicism growing up. A cousin in Perth has no idea either.

*

But what happened to me, several decades ago? A veneration of … what? Mystery. A veering towards it like an ocean liner subtly altering course in the great ocean of life. Yet the destination was – is – unknown.

Once God was completely absent from my world. I was a pit-bull atheist, a sneerer. Yet occasionally I'd stumble

210

across a church service and just … sit, usually in some foreign place where none of the aberrant behaviour would be reported back. There was something all-calming about these illicit experiences. A leak through the veneer of aspirant coolness; a gentle drip, drip through the restless, anxious, often bleakly alone twenties. I felt 'righted' by these assignations, balmed.

Then London. Life greedy, busy, grasping. Andrew and I in a bedsit on Fleet Street, both on gruelling night shifts. He sensed I needed something else – an anchor. One day he walked me across to St Bride's (known as 'the writers' church' because of its Fleet Street location). For 2000 years its plot by the Thames has hosted buildings that have been coracles of solace for various peoples, various religions. I found myself regularly slipping into its Sunday Evensong; brought to a stillness by a spiritual enveloping from a service mostly sung. I felt calmed, lit. Those evenings were clean. The shining hours.

I don't go to church anymore. At times say no, it's ridiculous, I'm with that gentle atheist Alain de Botton on this one; tipping a hat to the graces within organised religion but not sucked in by them. But then, but then, sometimes, the heart-tug. At night, standing in a room filled with the sleep of the children, just … breathing them in. And a great warmth floods through me – an enormous, glittery, heart-swelling gratitude – and I'm closing my eyes in unstoppable thanks. It's there again, in the wild places, where the silence hums. Antarctica's ice desert, central Australia's sand desert, under a full butter moon. Again, yes. Sometimes, often, I feel silted up by the great rambunctiousness of living; depleted. Need the cleanness of a religious way, a tuning fork back into calm.

Yet Elayn had none of this. She had nothing to look forward to in the end, just a release into the void. She craved it.

Living had become that hard.

22

I've been knocked down so many times I can't remember the numberplates but now, for the first time, it feels so hard to pick myself up. This is Nervous Breakdown. Retreating from the world. Trying to knead out a new wrinkle in the forehead from scrunching it up and being unable to; even in the middle of the night, in restless sleep. Talking in company then bringing myself up abrupt – they hate me, can't do this properly anymore, feel a fraud. Cannot exist in a professional space nor a private one; I need to dissolve this state. Is there a fix for grief? No. It's too private, too singular. A grubby, growly, secret pit I cannot climb out of. Why is it taking so long? Constable B might as well have said, on that day she came to my house, 'You will never recover.' 'You are now stepping into a new existence.' 'You will ask questions about this for the rest of your life.' What is needed: some process of alerting the world around me that I've travelled off into a secret land and will remain there for some time. And need everyone's forgiveness for it.

*

I write one of my newspaper columns from deep in bewilderment's pit, asking whether Elayn's actions were despair or empowerment. It receives the most responses I've ever had to any of my columns. It turns out there are a lot of Elayns out there.

*

'Your Mum's final act was bravery, pure bloody bravery on her behalf. Why? Because seven years ago when I was diagnosed with breast cancer I made a pact with myself that if it ever comes back I am not doing "terminal". No hospice, no wailing family and friends. I will simply pull the plug. I have the plan. It's a secret to everyone except one. My man knows and understands this and agrees he would do the same. We are both ex nurses. We know what the end entails, whether it be mental or physical problems, or in some cases both. Palliative care is not for me. All I have promised him is that it won't be him who finds my body.'

Name withheld

*

'My mother passed away in palliative care. She was there for seven weeks. She would have elected to go at three.

214

Instead we stared at her for the full seven not wanting to say our goodbyes … She was in enormous pain … so were we. Soul-destroying stuff. Let's hope the message gets out there that we are not talking about taking life, we're talking about releasing it.'

Sherelle Scott – Noosa QLD

*

'It was a choice your mother made, when she could. I wade through a sea of wheelchair-bound, demented, voiceless, amputated, broken old women (they are mostly women) as I visit my mother in a nursing home. She's increasingly less able to make any sense of her surroundings. Me. Her life. And I often arrive at dinner time, to that suffocating pungent smell of old-fashioned institutional cooking. How I loathe it. I rarely see any other visitors, and still wonder why. Perhaps your mother just weighed things up and made a very sensible decision. I can well imagine the lure of that, as I see my own fate over the horizon.'

Paul Mabarrack – Blackwood SA

*

'I also suffer from chronic, agonising, never easing, peripheral neuropathy of the sensory nerves of both feet which is seriously affecting my enjoyment of life. I have

215

a good GP and have had all the tests by neurologists, and have tried nearly every recommended medication, but to no avail – the chronic pain persists every second I'm awake. It really gets me down and I'm sure nobody fully understands the horrible impact it has on my life. Sometimes I get onto the internet and look up things like peripheral neuropathy and suicide – but that's not an option for me – I know that for sure. However I fully understand how your dear mother must have felt when she decided to euthanise herself – chronic pain can leave a person feeling absolutely miserable. I spoke to my doctor recently and said the pain is so severe I feel like having both feet amputated but of course that is not realistic, and also phantom pain apparently can be very painful after amputations. One of the main problems I face is that I feel nobody fully understands how much constant pain I am in, and there is no use whinging to people anyway.

'I look for a couch to lie on every five minutes and yet the chronic pain still fully nags at my mind every minute I lie on that couch. I am writing to you because I care that your dear mother finally decided her chronic pain was too unbearable to continue with and her decision was right for her – nobody else would really, fully, understand. I do.'

Name withheld

*

216

'Pain is considered by most medical practitioners as a complication and an irritation to all, rather than a medical entity to understand and manage. The outcome of poor pain management is all too self-evident. We as health professionals MUST do better. Much of our practice lacks evidence-based science, hence doctors continue past practices of inadequate pain management. Those practising in pain medicine utilise patient information, mindfulness, behavioural changes, education and understanding; appropriate physical activity protocols; and medications to attempt to manage a person's pain. It is somewhat unfortunate that many in health services disciplines still consider pain as somewhat incidental to disease/injury in the community. Many of my colleagues do not take pain (particularly persisting pain) seriously enough to take time with the sufferer to explain the issue and offer options. Public health and private medicine are getting their act together, but funding remains an issue when competing with the glamour clinical disciplines for the ever shrinking budget. And no, surgery is not always the answer ...'

Name withheld (an occupational & environmental physician)

*

'As an occupational therapist who treats people with chronic pain I have heard too many tragic stories like those of your mother. "Going under the knife" to correct a complex pain problem is all too often the first course of action suggested to people. Frequently though, surgery compounds the problem and spreads the pain even further than the original site of damage. The less aggressive options; helping the body realign itself through gentle exercises and movement, education on how to manage the pain better, or simply changing footwear before too many imbalances have occurred is invariably the far wiser and more effective choice. Bravo for the good old Blundstone … Chronic pain is called the "Invisible Epidemic" for good reason.'

Jane Muirhead – Perth WA

*

'My deepest sympathies, although your story is repeated every day for countless old people with ailments that can't be fixed. Their bodies have simply worn out and the medical profession flock to them, particularly if they are cashed up. Palliative care specialists love them in a semi-vegetative comatose state in a morphine haze, costing the community thousands per week just to keep these poor souls alive with little or no dignity left. My father who has just died barely avoided this fate, but my mother, who died of Alzheimer's, didn't. The last time I saw her, a frail, sad wraith, with no speech at all, few teeth left and no appetite was in the very last stages of wasting away, waiting for God, but the consultant orthodontist at the nursing home asked my permission to make her a full set of dentures, ($1500 in 1992). I refused, returned interstate and she died naturally seven days later. What happened to "duty of care" and "firstly, do no harm"?'

Richard van der Molen – Melbourne, VIC & Dodges Ferry, TAS

*

'I'm a Lifeline crisis counsellor. I've listened to many struggling with life. I often listen to paralysed people, with not one single moving muscle, locked inside their bodies, with no cognitive impairment, "talking" through mechanical voices. Poor buggers couldn't take their lives if they wanted to. When I haven't heard from them for a while, I quietly, guiltlessly hope that they've died, only to be disappointed when I get one of them on the phone again. Of the 2500 or so Australians who take their lives p.a. the highest age-specific category is males over eighty-five. These men never ring Lifeline. I can only think that they're resolute, and comfortable with their decision. And why not? More than likely they've lived full and productive lives. Their partner is probably gone, their own health in decline. For this group there are only a few years/months left. Why should they live according to others' expectations?

'Is it a right to take one's life? I believe it is/should be. I reckon your mum was empowered. When people have made up their minds they are often light of spirit, and relieved that whatever suffering they are enduring is about to end. I hope she led a wonderful life. And the older you get, the closer to her in deep spirit you might become. What a good thing!'

Rainer Jozeps – Adelaide SA

*

'The attitude (of your mother) would be that she must do whatever was "necessary" and it must be her final responsibility. She'd accept things must be done alone; the sort of attitude that, as the saying goes, "every heart knows its own sorrow." So you couldn't really enter into her feelings and she wouldn't altogether want it either; she'd just hope, even expect, you'd understand. There was neither pure selfishness nor pure motherly love in the action, just doing what seemed realistic and practical.'

Rollan McCleary – Queensland

*

'While it is hard for you to come to terms with your mum choosing to end her life on her terms and with dignity, I understand the position that she was in. She was in pain and struggled on a daily basis with no end to her suffering. You mention that she did not want to be placed in a nursing home – who does? I plan to make a "graceful exit" when my time comes. I was diagnosed with young-onset Parkinson's disease ten years ago at the age of forty-three. Before this life-changing diagnosis I was working full time in a job that I loved. I had a wonderful life with my husband and two children, who were thirteen and eighteen at the time. When I was diagnosed, I promised myself that I would go on living my life to the fullest until such time as life became too much of a daily struggle then I would make a "graceful exit".

'My first "graceful exit" came in 2012 when I had to cease working due to worsening Parkinson's symptoms. There is a large cohort of people living with young-onset Parkinson's disease and our biggest fear is rotting away in a nursing home before we are even sixty-five years old. I know of several people from my support group who are now in nursing homes and they are in their fifties. So for many of us euthanasia is the only way out when the daily struggle with Parkinson's disease becomes too much. My mum and dad had to spend their final years in a nursing home and I witnessed their misery on a daily basis. Mum had a stroke that left her bedridden and force-fed five times/day by PEG feeding (tube inserted into the stomach); and Dad had vascular dementia – which for him was total torture, being locked up like a prisoner. He starved himself to death. Many brave doctors and nurses will call this for what it is – futile care. There is no hope of a cure or a return to quality of life.

'People in chronic pain and with incurable diseases simply want a choice in how to end their life. There are some people who may well choose to go into a nursing home, but for most it's a living hell. When I can no longer carry out "activities of daily living and personal hygiene" I do not want to be reliant on care-givers and a burden to my children. Your mum made a "graceful exit" on her terms (empowerment) and because she did not want to be a burden (motherly love) – it was her life and her choice. There is a tsunami of people out there who will choose this path, whether it is legal or not.'

Gaye Hargreaves – Dunsborough, WA

*

'We share so many similarities surrounding our mother's deaths. My mother, like yours, chose to end her own life, on her own terms. Exit International, the Voluntary Euthanasia Society et al, exist for the strong. My mum was a strong, intelligent woman for whom independence was everything. She developed intractable pain as a result of a fall, and like your mum, a slow and steady decline meant that a return to any level of comfort was highly unlikely. As one who has gone through what you are right now, I know the following to be true: you will feel sometimes like you are seven years old. Vulnerable and small and infinitely empty. But your children will help you to keep busy and not dwell too much on your sadness. There is always a meal to cook, washing to hang out or some domestic task calling your name. And you will reflect on the way she died and ask yourself, "Was she lonely?" "Why didn't she tell me?" Maternal protectiveness continues no matter how old the mother.'

Name Withheld

*

'My fabulous father has expressed similar views about nursing homes, and the "DNR" form, displayed as a solitary pinning on the kitchen fridge, should spur me to … what? Our wonderful, proud parents are of a generation who lived with appreciation, and by a sense of duty. I've no doubt your dear mother loved fiercely, and would be so proud of you for highlighting, even in grief, a pressing need to investigate legal options for families further.'

Sue Walker – Adelaide SA

*

'Your mother's choice. That's it. To rail against that … does it disrespect her last act of self-determination?'

Lorraine Meades – Bendigo VIC

*

'The politics are a bottomless swamp. If "oldies" were allowed to go peacefully – surrounded by loving family, entirely voluntarily, when it all became unbearable for them – then all hell would break loose. The reduced demand for old-age palliative care would cause massive unemployment. Surgeons would lose about half of their opportunities to do lucrative operations, funded by the taxpayer. Modern medicine started by keeping us alive when we had so many productive years ahead of us, and we were grateful for the chance to do all the things we wanted to do. Now medicine too often keeps us alive long after we have done all the things we want to achieve, and are dreading even one more day, more than ready to go.'

Mike and Maddy – Mandurah WA

*

'We feel very sorry for both you and your mum ... She obviously knew the whole ghastly draconian legal situation and kept you in ignorance for your own sake. We need politicians with the backbone to change the legislation concerning euthanasia. I also have fairies at the bottom of the garden ... We are sorry you didn't manage to pick up on your mother's research – We think that her final moments were more than an act of empowerment. She was certainly taking control of her life and the way it ended in a dignified manner. She was a brave and resourceful person, who need not have been alone as she died. It is not illegal to be present as a person takes their life; only if you assist them in any way to die. But perhaps she doubted that family members or friends would love her enough to "let her go" and would make it simple for you all. So chin up girl! She is better off than living in unrelieved pain.'

'Two Hillbillies from the West' – WA

*

'My husband did the same thing. Long-term heart disease then the diagnosis of a very advanced cancer threw him into the willing arms of the medical fraternity who don't know when to stop. No one ever suggested he do nothing; just live and spend time with those he loved. Overwhelmed with guilt at not recognising what he was planning, I eventually consulted with a psychologist who cautioned me to not judge, that given the right circumstance, we are all capable of suicide. His note still haunts me: "What a disgrace. You will find what remains of me in the canal. I cannot burden you with the impending mire."

'Empowerment, despair, selfishness? Some of each; unwittingly they pass their burden on to us. It took years to forgive him but I have. Hold your mum's memory close to your heart; I have no doubt she did what she thought was best for everyone. I've several friends who have their end mapped out; they will not linger and I suspect there's much of this that doesn't reach the press … we reach our "use by date" and don't want the indignity of long term illness.'

Name withheld

*

'Nikki, you can't blame yourself because your mother wanted to end her life in her way and a way in which she was in control. We would all like to have that power when the time comes.'

Margaret Deacon – Gold Coast QLD

*

'I did want to offer my small insight into my mother's attempt to kill herself, during her battle with cancer. She died in 2013, in a nursing home, she had given up, couldn't walk or care for herself and just shut down and died. The cancer (in her brain) wasn't the cause, she just decided she didn't want to be here anymore. Her illness had been a long one.

'Like you I have often thought about what I said, did etc. and tried to understand my mother's years during her illness. I do remember that when she said to me that she was going to kill herself I didn't believe her. Like your mother she took an overdose but my father found her and she was rushed to hospital. My abiding memory of this is how furious she was with my father and I that we didn't let her die. She had had enough and everything that she valued was being taken away from her, most importantly her fierce independence. Now others were intruding upon her, others were making the decisions and she hated it. Strangely I understood why she wanted to die and I respected this, despite my devastation at that thought. I believe that the illness had taken everything, all decision making and dignity was gone, the only thing my mother had left was her ability to choose to die. I'm not sure if it is selfishness, love etc., as you ask. For me these are not questions I've needed to ask myself because as her carer, with a long illness, it was all too obvious – what else did she have control of?'

Wendy Bertrand-Clark – Traralgon VIC

*

'I know you will be sharing every daughter's feelings of love/guilt etc. for so many years to come. The only comfort I can offer you is this. I am now seventy-three, and I would definitely choose the same path as your mother/my father, when push comes to shove. Because the older I get, the more I appreciate that my life is all – and I, and I alone, hold it in my hands. My life, my choice as to how I live it, or decide to end it.'

Helen Brierty – Yandina, QLD

*

'You've reminded me that my wife Rachel and I need to be listening to not only our parents' words but also to their subtext as they too wrestle with the loss of independence, the loss of control, the loss of dignity that comes with chronic pain and the aging process. We need to not allow ourselves to become frustrated by their reluctance to ask for our help so as not to be a burden on their children and families. We too have felt confused, hesitant, impotent and unsure of what to do; you've encouraged us to be up-front, to speak straight and without hesitancy to understand what they are actually feeling.'

Paul Wappett – Melbourne VIC

*

'Pain has changed my mother, not just physically but mentally. She has become cranky and often cruel in her behaviour, especially towards my father and me. It is possibly a reaction to her pain although my children and even my father tell me that she was always critical of others. Perhaps, her terrible pain has altered her. Whether she will

228

be able to heal completely will be something that we will have to wait to see.'

Ruma Chakravarti – Adelaide SA

*

'Your story about the passing of your mum reminded me of the passing of my dad. He wanted to "do it" himself but needed my help as he could not leave the house. (He had joined the Euthanasia Society.) He collected the sleeping tablets; I provided the mortar and pestle from the Uni Lab and I bought his favourite bottle of Malt Scotch. I waited with dread at finding him dead with a plastic bag over his face (still gives me the creeps sixteen years later). Next day I turned up to find an empty bottle and a very drunk old man ... this happened a further five times! He said he just couldn't do it as he was afraid he would end up a vegetable if things went awry.'

Name withheld

*

'If it's any help – after two serious bouts of cancer/ chemo/radiation and god awful pains – I contacted Exit International with the desire to end it. I looked on death as the end of pain – peace and escape. But my husband worked tirelessly at keeping me alive to a degree that was heroic.

So I changed my mind. I had to live for someone else as he was not ready for a lonely life. My motto was "Someone or something to love. Something to do. Something to look forward to." And that made it easy for me.'

Lurline Frank

*

'You are not alone, and by sharing your story, you enable more people to come forward and share their stories; particularly, but not exclusively, women. After all, they are still the carers and nurturers in our society.'

Irene Goldwasser – St Kilda VIC

*

'The whole euthanasia issue is not going to go away, but one has the impression many people in high places are trying to dampen it down. If more females were shaping our laws, I don't think this would be the case. Women in general are the carers of the frail and dying. Men, in general, aren't nearly as involved. I'm now an elderly person, and myself and female friends have found our husbands aren't at all interested in discussing end of life arrangements. My husband says he doesn't want to discuss it and to do whatever I want when the time comes.'

Rosalie Barry – Tewantin QLD

*

'I too feel guilty about not listening more to a loved one in distress and worse, being too tied up in my own issues to notice. Even twenty-nine years after my beautiful twenty-five-year-old son committed suicide I still beat myself up over what I didn't do and what I could have done if I had known more. I have learnt strategies to keep myself sane which has kept me going, and knowing our loved ones are no longer suffering helps. Your mum was a beautiful woman and deserved better from doctors. It's almost as if they killed her. I'm so pleased you shared your heartbreaking story as it may well save a life by making people more aware of others in deep despair, and point them to where help is available.'

Elaine Joseph – Gold Coast QLD

*

'I know how you feel. Yes, you will never recover from the loss; and perhaps a perverse sense, even, of abandonment/desertion; I felt that but I was much younger, twenty-eight. Hug your children.'

Suzanne Edgar – ACT

*

'You mentioned "selfishness" – a strategic observation because it links with "rejection". During my twenty-eight years as a mental health practitioner, rejection was often cited as a feeling experienced by those left behind. When your mum died in those circumstances lots of kin would have felt let down – it's an understandable emotion. They say we spend most of our lives trying to live up to our perception of parental expectations, so it cuts to the quick when Mum or Dad choose to leave this life alone.'

Mike Fenton – South West of WA

*

'We all try to examine the historical events and how we might have done better and it isn't easy. In my case the memory of my mother passing didn't need examination, but I'm often conscious of the time I asked her, when I was angry at something now irrelevant, some six decades ago, "Do you love me?" She looked at me with a very sad face and a tear rolled out as she said, "Don't you know?" Ashamed was I for the rest of my life.'

George – South Fremantle

*

'I have just come back from Holland. My younger sister, Annelies, was at the final stage of cancer and had the opportunity to end her life with the help of a doctor. She was so happy! She did not yet suffer too much, she used marijuana to keep nausea at bay and it helped her sleep too. She was totally clear headed and very ready to leave this world. She had had a long and interesting life, with many people who loved her and felt inspired by her.

'Your mother chose to die because she didn't think her life gave her the dignity and independence she wanted, needed. Dying is not a decision you take lightly. What you tell us in your writing is that she planned it carefully, with as little impact or nasty surprises as possible.

'Thank her for that. That she did not tell you, is, no doubt, because she loved you too much, knew you'd run into trouble if she did. Dying is a lonely act. Though we were with my sister (three close friends, two sisters) my sister still died all alone. But you should have seen her smile when she got her injection. She was so happy. No more pain, no more travelling slowly and painfully to an end of life in a way that negated her independence and enjoyment of a very good and rich life.

'Annelies was a very intelligent and independent woman. Quality of life was most important. And so, when she heard that the cancer had come back and was spreading, she talked to her doctor. She'd known my sister for a long time and agreed to be the one to give Annelies her injection. Then Annelies had to go to an independent psychiatrist, who talked with her, checked that her illness was terminal and gave her his permission for the procedure. And then, when she was too tired to take care of herself, and decided she wanted to leave, she had to start the actual procedure, and made a phone call. An unknown doctor visited her to assess her health and suffering. That's rather ironic, who can assess other people's suffering? Yet, such are the rules and regulations. And so …

'In Holland the procedure is not legal, but it is not prosecuted if the rules are followed.'

Frieda van Aller – Port Douglas QLD

*

Receiving the deluge of reader letters helped me to understand, buoyed me; suddenly, I did not feel so alone. I wish Elayn had had a swell of voices around her – myriad voices of understanding and compassion – in her bleakest hours. She didn't. It felt like she was unbearably isolated, and frightened, and floundering.

One letter, in particular, tugged.

23

'Dear Nikki

'Your words hit me right in the heart. You see, I'm on the other side of the page. I'm a woman, mother and doctor, and I'm planning to go to Switzerland next year to take the option of assisted suicide with Dignitas International.

'I'm sixty-one, and have been suffering from a disabling, progressive and very painful form of arthritis for the last twenty-three years. Although I don't know the details of your mum's circumstances, I suspect that the major differences between us are that I'm a doctor, and I have enough money to access a service overseas which I believe should be available for all people who need it. I made the decision to end my life at the time of my choosing five years ago, after a very painful and unsuccessful operation. Since then I've spent every day wrestling with the terrible balance between when my pain became too much to bear, and when my children would be sufficiently launched into their lives that they could manage without me (I'm a sole parent). I was hoping to wait until sixty-five, but the continuing encroachment of greater disability and decreasing effectiveness of my pain management regime (I've been fortunate to have the help of a chronic pain clinic, and lucky to avoid abuse of my opiate medication, although it's a daily temptation) has forced my hand.

'My children have known of my decision since I made it five years ago. Last Christmas I told them that this would be my last full year, and that I planned to make it the best year for all of us since I first got sick. I'm going to access some of my superannuation funds, and do something special with each of them this year. My eldest and I are off to Africa next month. I know that whatever I do with them will result in more pain, but it will be worth it for the pleasure of giving us all special memories of this final year together.

'Of course, every day I feel guilty for being such a coward and leaving them early. On the other hand, I want to leave them all a good inheritance, rather than spending the next twenty years using up the money that I've saved for them in supporting myself as my life continues to contract around me. I know they'll miss me terribly, but they have watched me suffer for a long, long time, and understand my need to end that suffering. I still enjoy lots of things I do in life, but as I explained to my physiotherapist, those things are like icing on a shit-cake. The icing is great, but it's still shit underneath – and the icing gets thinner every day.

'I would dearly love to be able to carry out my wishes here in Australia with all my family around me, and as a doctor I would certainly be able to access the appropriate drugs. But what then? If my children were with me, they would be subject to investigation by the authorities. If I were alone, then someone would have the traumatic experience of finding my body, and the children would then have to identify me. I can't subject people to this. It's a travesty that in a free, secular country, people like your mother and I are proscribed from having control over the time and method of our passing. I don't know if it helps you hearing my story, but perhaps it might give you some insight into how it feels on the other side.

*

The letter was from Dr Helena Thompson (not her real name). I've never approached, in person, any of the thousands of my column readers who've written to me over the years. With Helena, for the first time, I take a leap of faith and get in touch with her. It's like stepping – fearfully – through a door I've never had a need to go through, and have never wanted to. Who knows what's on the other side.

*

Life. A woman determined to extract every last bit of joy that she can out of her time on this earth. And she's only got a year or so left.

Helena's home is two hours away. Before setting out to visit a complete stranger I write her details on a slip of paper and leave it on my desk, for Andrew, in case I never return. Who says this reader is really a doctor? Even a woman? A Google search tells me such a doctor exists, but maybe it's one of the nutter-haters who's used her name to lure me. These are just some of the charming responses to my writing I've received on social media: 'As if I'd trust an article written by something that bleeds for a week every month and doesn't die.' 'I hope you die alone. Cold. Afraid.' 'An alpha male doesn't care what women think.' 'I just want big tits and to be left the **** alone when I've blown.' Yet I leap.

*

Helena lives in a house teetering on the edge of a bush gully in the shadow of a great mountain. I know instantly she's what I've needed. Grief is a silent, secret, confounding world, and she knows it.

*

Like Elayn, vivacity defines her. Helena hoots with laughter, shines with raucous joy. Her voice is clear, expressive,

238

intelligent. Her short grey hair is coloured in playful rainbow stripes. This is a woman who knows how to live, fearlessly. It's in her clothes, voice; her open face with its roguish smile. She's known the underbelly of life, which gives her great empathy. She now works in drug and alcohol dependency after doctoring in emergency care, psychiatry and prison healthcare. Her gift is compassion, and she knows that not all doctors have it.

*

Helena wants my story first up. Listening is her job and life. Understanding, processing, helping. 'As a doctor, the most important thing is to share your humanity as a fellow human being – and to make people laugh. I'm old [she doesn't seem it], and I think old age is a wonderful thing because if you allow yourself to keep learning it teaches you. You never stop learning. Terence, the Roman playwright, said, "I am human, and nothing of that which is human is alien to me." As a doctor you must make every patient, no matter what they're telling you, feel like they're part of humanity. You mustn't allow them to feel that what they're telling you is weird or odd, whatever it may be. And that's why being in pain is so helpful as a doctor, because you can share the understanding with your patients, and the desperate temptation to have more opiates every single day because they make you feel good. Taking drugs is a normal part of managing the huge gap between what we hope life is going to be, and what life is. It's not criminal or evil, it's normal. But then people get caught up, and it overtakes their world.'

*

She's had twenty-three years of living with chronic pain. I do not want to fall in love with this woman, knowing how the year will end for her. But I cannot help it. Our conversation roams over days, weeks, months; she visits me at my home for a long Sunday lunch about pain and motherhood and letting go and life; she can manage it because she is heavily dosed up with her opioids. Responsibly dosed up.

'I got a viral infection in the nerves of my chest wall (in my late thirties). I was very sick. It left me with severe chronic nerve pain in a band around my chest. It turned on a gene I already had for a kind of generalised osteoarthritis. This ran in my family. It's become more and more severe as time goes on. I've had operations on both hands. Two bones cut out of my hands. Four hip replacements, three major operations on my back, and innumerable injections to joints everywhere from a finger to my back, to the upper back, lower back, joints around my hip, and the muscles and tendons because I get tendonitis as well. I've got severe nerve pain down both legs, which has become worse after every operation. I've still got severe pain in the chest wall. I've got arthritis in what they call the facet joints down my back. I've had a cyst in my back that was pressing on my spinal cord. I've had tendonitis in my hips and pelvis and arm. Basically it's just very widespread, severe, getting-worse pain. No way out. I've had nerves to the facet joints kind of burnt off with radio waves. I went through that last year. It didn't make any difference.

'Every time something else happens it's another step towards disability. It's never getting better. I'd be ending up in a wheelchair. I'm very close to permanent wheelchair territory. And once you get past a certain level of disability, you don't want to be like that anymore.'

*

Like Elayn, Helena is a beautiful woman who takes pride in her appearance. 'The vanity stuff kills you when you have chronic pain. The first thing I noticed was that I was never able to sleep on my side anymore, and that was twenty-three years ago. Then it was that I could no longer wear a bra. I've had to give all my beautiful clothes away. Can't wear anything around my back. And no high heels. For a woman, every time you get to a new level of disability, you have to change your look. You can't manage long hair because it hurts to lift your arms. Can't manage fancy makeup because it's difficult to put things on. All these little things bring you down an extra level.' Elayn spent her final year being brought down, and then further down.

*

Helena is sexy and earthy. Quick to joy. She, like Elayn, looks like a woman who'd love laughing in bed. Yet there will be no partner by her side for this final journey. 'When I split up with my youngest child's dad twenty years ago I made a decision not to look for another relationship. My kids deserved all my attention, and I didn't want them involved with any other father figure. They'd already had enough of that [she's had three marriages]. So I concentrated on them until their teens. By then my pain was so severe that I realised I didn't have enough energy to look for love. And I could no longer do evenings. All I can do is go to bed. So I haven't been in a relationship – or even on a date – for twenty years.'

*

Pain has leaked its way into all corners of Helena's life. 'You have to choose where you're going to work because some place, well, the chair isn't comfortable enough. My definition of a good place to have coffee is absolutely somewhere with a comfy chair. The right chair at home is the only place where I don't have to think about where I'm sitting. There's also teeth. My pain is so severe that I clench them all the time. And all the opiates I take make them brittle, so they break with alarming regularity. I'm always off to the dentist; and in terms of vanity the front ones have been ground down so far they've required building up.'

*

Then there's sleep, which also affected Mum. She was sleeping in my own childhood bed near the end, trying to get herself comfortable. Some days it was hard to get her up. She was sleeping a lot in the four days before her death. Helena explains that her own capacity to sleep has gone down dramatically: 'I have to make sure the pillows are right so that all the various pains are balanced. I put a pain-relieving gel on my elbow. A knee supporter on my leg to make it warm and a hot water bottle next to it. There's a pillow under each arm. I have to put patches on my chest walls. My back is itchy. I have a back scratcher in my bed. I might have to put steroid cream on my hands. And I can't take sleeping pills every night because you get tolerant to them too fast. So I only take them on the two days I have to get up early to go to work. Then with sleep, because there's always some level of pain, I wake up every sixty or ninety minutes or so. It's so wearying. And there's always the temptation to take more sleeping tablets or painkillers. It never works out well, especially with the sleeping tablets, because if you take them a few days in a row they stop working – and of course there's always the guilt about asking your doctor for more.

'Although your mum ended up doctor shopping, I'm sure she felt shame and guilt about it every time. I feel that too, each time I see my GP for regular medications, even though rationally I know my requests aren't excessive. How much worse it must have been for her. And taking so many medications – I take more than twenty a day – it must have been so easy to get confused and forget how much she'd taken on any one day.'

With Helena, I'm piecing together a portrait of a chronic pain sufferer. How it takes over every part of a person's life. Like weeds, that in the end are impossible to pull out.

*

Helena is disciplined with her pill regime. 'There are two keys to managing chronic pain. First, managing it not on how you feel today, but on a reliable, thought-out basis. What you take is regular pain relief, not pain relief based on how you feel on a particular day. You're not responding to the pain, you have to regulate it. The other key is that you must expect enormous variability. Since I came back from my holiday in Africa, well, it was such a great rest that my pain has been better. And I'm thinking oh, oh, maybe it's going to be all right. But that's what pain does. Sometimes it gets better for a while – but then it goes back to what it was. Over twenty-three years I've learnt that every so often I'm going to get a dip. And then I'm going to have to change my whole life based on that dip. The first dip was when I realised I wouldn't be able to lift up toddlers anymore. The second dip was when I realised I'd never be able to work in Emergency anymore. And the trouble with being on opiates all the time is two things. One, you have to abide by all the rules. What dose you're on and what you're allowed to be on, and two, you've got to deal with the daily temptation to use more.'

I ask Helena if she's more disciplined, as a doctor.

'No. I guess I'm just fortunate to have avoided being an addictive personality. That's pure luck. Most people who've been on opiates for twenty-three years would have developed an addiction. Specially people who like them. I find opiates wonderful drugs. Not only do they relieve pain, they give me energy. As you can see today, I've got plenty.'

She does. She's enjoying her champagne, helping with food preparation at my kitchen counter, holding regal court at the dining table. Too alive for a too-soon death. 'I've doubled up my OxyContin today. It's the one that's seen as an evil drug, that your mum took. It's just a long-acting opiate. When I first went on it, I said to the pain specialist, I don't understand this, these give me energy, they don't sedate me. He said that's what happens with patients who have chronic pain – it wakes them up. Usually they're exhausted because they're distracted by the pain. But suddenly, they're not exhausted.'

Elayn. Immediately after her foot operation. Euphoric. And I had no idea what this new lightness would lead to. Assumed, naïvely, she was now on her way out of pain's grip.

*

Helena's body has developed a tolerance to the drugs, yet she's physically dependent on her opiates. 'Every single day I have to wrestle with temptation to take extra doses, because they're so bloody good. They're fantastic drugs if used appropriately. But they wear off after a while. Everything does. I'm on a higher dose than I was twenty-three years ago yet I've never become addicted. But it's a daily thing. When I go to bed I think, 'Shall I take an extra dose of oxycodone?' As someone with chronic pain they're fabulous. Not only do they make you feel good but they get rid of the pain. It would be so easy as a doctor to take too much. When I take a pill at bedtime, I think, is this being an addict? I think about that every single night.'

*

According to Helena, there's a big difference between dependency and addiction:

'Being dependent doesn't matter – physical dependency is when your body knows it needs that extra opiate to continue to function. Addiction starts when it takes over your life. When you go out of your way to take extra tablets. When you start lying to your doctor about how much you're having. When you doctor shop because you need that high even more than you need the pain relief.'

Helena tells me, bluntly, that Elayn was an addict.

*

I ask her if any of her four children – aged twenty-one to forty – have said to her along the way, don't do it Mum, don't kill yourself.

'Oh, they've been too nice for that,' she laughs.

'They haven't tried to talk you out of it?'

'No. My first hip replacement was a disaster. I tried to sue the hospital but it didn't work because I couldn't get anyone else in the medical profession to support me in saying it was negligence. I ended up with devastating nerve pain down both legs. It was poorly treated, and that's when I decided I was going to die when I was sixty-five.

'I'm sixty-one now so I've had to give up earlier than I hoped. The kids have known what's going on all the way along. An operation last year didn't work. That's what made me decide that this is it, I'm going to have fun with my kids this year.' The shine of her roguish smile.

247

*

'How will your children cope?'

'That's my biggest problem. I'm hurting them. Every day I think, am I being selfish? As opposed to how they're going to feel better because they know what I'm going through. It's really hard.'

*

The difference between Helena's family and my own is that hers has communicated, and over a long period. The children have been with her, closely, every step of this difficult journey. 'I don't think they're going to feel rejected. They're going to miss me, dreadfully. They're all very close, and we love each other a lot, and that's the worst part. On the other hand they know this is going to get worse. They've seen it over twenty-three years. They understand why I'm doing it.'

My family were amateurs at this euthanasia business, floundering in the dark.

*

'Yes, the kids would prefer to have me rather than my money. But I want to leave them what I didn't have. My parents were poor – and I want them to be in a position

248

that they're never going to have to worry. If I sit around getting more crippled and less able to do anything I'm not going to leave them the legacy I want to leave them. Which is the capacity to do what they want, without having to worry financially.

'There's always amazing stuff [to be experienced, that Helena will miss out on by ending it all] but if you want to have an incredible year you've got to overdose on all your medication. I've been so careful for so many years. You can't do that on an ongoing basis, but I think if I was going to have one year that's a huge gift to the kids, then the way to do it is to take whatever medication it requires so they won't be worried about me having fun. But it's not something you can do every year, because you're going to be stuck at the end of it having had more medication than is appropriate. I'm already on a higher dose of opiates than anyone's supposed to have. And if I just kept on trying to have another good year, a) it would use up too much money, and b) I would end up on too much medication. Then I'd have problems with my GP, and my own management. So if I was doing this for more than a year I'd be doing nothing but getting myself into trouble.'

*

Helena's children are going to Switzerland to be with her at the end, as is her best friend.

'You have to be a member of Dignitas International, based in Zurich. The plan is to have a nice little trip first, then go. I can't organise it more than three months beforehand because you have to have a medical examination, by your own doctor, which is three months or less before the deed. It will be saying, yes I know that this person is suffering from either terminal illness or unmanageable pain, and yes, this person is not depressed.'

You do not have to have a terminal illness to die through Dignitas. A lot of documentation is required. Not only passports, medical records, specialist medical records and driver's licence, but statements from family members like children and grandchildren. Then family members who've travelled to Switzerland with the person who wants to die may be interviewed by Dignitas, and sometimes several times over. It's a lengthy, thorough process of approval.

'They won't let you do it if you're acutely depressed, because the whole point is to say that this is a decision you're making in sound mind. If you're severely depressed you're not making a decision in sound mind. My doctor's not keen on it, he's very fond of me. But he knows I made this decision five years ago, and when the time comes up he'll be writing a letter saying I'm of sound mind, and that this is a long-term thing – not a sudden impulse towards suicide. When you go over there you get examined by their doctors as well. You've got to have someone with you, you can't do it all by yourself.'

A camera records the final moments in case police need to investigate. No doctor is present. A first drink is taken – an anti-vomiting drug. It needs half an hour to take effect, a time that can be deeply stressful. Dignitas staff then put a drink containing Nembutal on a table. That final drink is not handed by staff to the person who wishes to die; they must pick up the glass themselves. A doctor isn't allowed to administer a lethal injection. It's entirely up to the individual, and they're asked right until the final moment if they want to change their mind.

'You take one drink that stops you from being nauseated,' Helena explains, 'then you have the barbiturate drink – and just go to sleep. That's all you do.'

Simple. Easy. Devastating. But less devastating to her family and friends than if she had decided to take her own life without warning, consolation or explanation. As Elayn did to us.

*

There is something deeply stable within Helena, she has an inner reserve of strength and discipline. I'm falling deeper in love with her seductive magnificence, and it is almost unbearable that shortly she will no longer be with us. Helena, who is so alive, yet so ready for a thoughtful death.

I ask her if some of her children are having long dark nights of the soul. 'Probably. They won't tell me. But they have seen how much worse I've gotten over the years, and they suffer when I suffer. All the time.'

And yet, and yet. Nothing is set in stone. My heart leaps.

'Dignitas has had experience of people changing their minds. It's not exactly a lock-in contract. And it's expensive. The biggest problem for me is that you have to be cremated. It costs a lot of money to bring the body home. Maybe I should be buried in Switzerland. I don't want my body's energy and protein wasted. I've always wanted to push up roses. My youngest is going to sculpt a marble angel over my grave.'

She looks across at him, he smiles in assent. With pain in his eyes.

*

'Do I believe in an afterlife? I don't know. As a scientist I don't believe in things unless the evidence is presented to me, although I remain open-minded. I've seen a lot of people die because I've been an emergency physician, and my impression is that people go somewhere. I always spoke to people in the re-sus room, and some of them hadn't left yet. Some of them didn't leave until their families came in. I could tell. I wondered where they'd gone. The older I got, I thought the more openly I could talk about this with other staff, and found that a lot – particularly middle-aged women – who worked in emergency felt the same way. They felt they would know when someone left, and when someone hadn't. And they would speak to them just like I do. But there's a conspiracy of silence. Medical practitioners don't want to talk about it because it seems so odd. So I suspect that people leave their ... containers ... and go somewhere. But I can't pretend to know because I have no faith.'

*

There is no absolute decision. The world may change and Helena with it.

'I want to make this year the best ever and so far it's been fabulous. But if I don't go through with Dignitas then I won't be able to work anymore, because of the increasing pain, which will be very hard. For years my GP's been saying to me, why are you still working? Because I love it. And I'm doing good. You get as much back from your patients as you give to them. It goes both ways.'

Oh yes, Helena's doing good.

24

The first Christmas after Elayn's death Paul is with us. For the first time in my children's lives. Drawing the family in close. It will always be this now. It works. We have learnt.

*

A long time after the funeral, what feels like too long, a phone call. Elayn's ashes need collecting from the crematorium. The official voice on the other end of the line is practised in its compassion towards the stranger.

The enormous complex on the fringes of Sydney's Botany Bay is a still, odd, removed place; a city of the dead with few signs of human inhabitation despite a full carpark. Gardens and roses and tiny plaques straddle a wide road. And most heartbreaking of all – a children's garden. Can't bear to look, dwell, read. My grief is nothing compared to this. It veers the trauma into perspective.

The administration building is all corporate efficiency and compassion. Promptly I'm ushered into a side room.

A woman asks for a signature on a release form, she wears a cloak of bureaucratic care. She's seen a lot of tears, it's in the careful set of her shoulders and the curve of her compassionate back. It's over in a few minutes. I'm out. With Elayn. Reduced to this. An oblong foam box. In a smart, shiny carrier like a shopping bag from a very expensive boutique. She'd approve of that. Make a joke. Yet I feel weighted with responsibility. What to do with her? Where was home for her? Need to get this right. Elayn is placed tenderly on the floor of the car in front of the toddler car seat.

Driving home, it feels like a suturing. We're together. We'll always be together now.

*

I've heard stories of people who've left their parents in the car to be constantly with them, of mothers in clothes cupboards, fathers in tool sheds. I can't seem to move Elayn's foam box from by the baby seat – she's with me as we drive, months later, and I'm always driving. Feel eccentric in my ease with all this; my mother my constant companion. When the car needs the mechanic for repairs I finally move her, to the kitchen. This is not right. Her home will be found. It is close to here, to us. Her world. Her vivacious life. We settle on a plaque in a sunny corner of a memorial garden overlooking the harbour, with gardenias in front of her and a tall blue sky above her. It feels right.

Boh's birthday. The first after Nonna's death. We're all apprehensive beforehand. Elayn had come to our house every child's birthday with cupcakes and a card with cash in it. Everyone loved the birthday visits – they sparkled us up, gathered us to the table for ceremony. This was the first children's birthday without her since we'd been back. Beforehand, it felt weighted, addled by absence.

Yours truly made the cake. Yep. For the first time in fifteen years of motherhood because previously, the supermarket had always let me off the hook. Baking was one of those things, like cooking casseroles and curries, I'd never bothered to tuck into the growing up. It worked. Picture my children's incredulity. My astonishment. I'll do this cake thing again, step into this domestic life, become a different mother. Bob is with us on the day, too. We insist. We mention Nonna but do not dwell on her; life is growing over us. We're moving on.

*

A small white box arrives from The Netherlands. Inside, snugly packed, are two thin plastic gloves, one double-sided syringe filled with epoxy resin, a paintbrush, four wooden spatulas and one tiny round jar of gold powder. A *Kintsugi* kit. Tips: 'Have some disposable wet wipes nearby if correction is desired.' 'Use the weight of gravity while waiting for the glue to set.' 'Use on almost any material you like.' I do. But this is for one material in particular.

*

The brittle bits of porcelain have been waiting for this moment for a long time. On the dining table, shattered pieces of ceramic are grouped into methodical piles. Edges pieced with edges. Slivers with shards. Assembling an intricate jigsaw. It takes days. And days.

Assembling and dismantling. Attempting, stopping. Beginning again. What is quickly learnt: it is no use beginning with two random pieces and gluing them together. You have to start from the bottom of the lanterns, the base widened by hard wax, and work your way up. Slowly, laboriously, lost in this world, pieces are glued together, some so beautifully you cannot discern the join. Others sit uncomfortably but that is so, part of the process; beauty in failure. I wait for two pieces to dry before adding another piece, then another, first-aiding each tiny porcelain tower. The world around me recedes. It is deeply satisfying, this repair of what seemed beyond repair. As the lanterns nudge towards completion the joins, more violently, do not match up. It will have to do. Let go, let go, there is strange beauty in this too. The beauty of imperfection, and an acceptance of it.

The poet Douglas Dunn urges us to look to the living, love them and hold on, only that. And in a world that seems like it's darkening irretrievably around us it feels like this is the most urgent thing we can do. Especially as parents. Most of all as parents, because we're confronted continually by our own raging sense of powerlessness and imperfection. There's power in the equation, of course, but so much more of a powerlessness in the parent–child relationship, especially as teenage children zoom into adulthood. All our flaws are laid bare to the child, for they see us at our most reduced. We do not want complexity in our parents, want fairy tale, vanilla. For in seeing their complexity we see ourselves – in all our frailty. See what we're in danger of becoming. I've spent a lifetime trying to understand Elayn's flaws. I see it more simply now. She was all too human. That is all. May my own children be wiser, and more forgiving.

Do all parents carry with them the weight of a nonexistent perfection that their children expect of them? An essential component of growing up is accepting the very human fallability of your parents. Only then can you become adult yourself.

*

All mothers say cruel and unnecessary things to their daughters in the heat of the moment. All mothers fling words later regretted. Elayn's problem was that from my teens all my frustrations and furies were recorded; my journal the tape recorder. The writer documents it. Elayn had no hope against the archivist, and knew it.

*

Parenting is bloody hard. Andrew and I are still learning, endlessly; and regret that our eldest is the one experimented on the most. We're feeling our way as each new stage of our son's youthful existence unfolds in all its stubbornness and vividness, its frustration and exhilaration and shout. He's blazing the trail for the rest and doesn't even know it. Boh is close behind him. Even now we're losing these two boy-men, who are, suddenly, too swiftly, on their own journeys. The complicated death of Nonna has catapulted them on to adulthood.

That roar of childhood, so brief. Heart in mouth we watch them. Hold them, when we can. But neither of them want it. They will only share so much of their worlds now. And it feels like the nub of me has never been more raw and exposed than as a parent. Everything hurts. The heart is wide open.

*

Parenthood feels like an endless process of shoring up the dam – as one area springs a leak you rush to patch it up and then there's another leak, and another; it's an endless process of soothing, sorting, fixing. Elayn, eventually, gave up on all that. At least with me. I disappointed her, embarrassed her; sometimes, it felt, to the exclusion of everything else. There are no sureties with parenthood, no matter how much (or little) you love. Who as a parent could guarantee that any of their children will never end up in an invidious position one day? The gutter, the brothel, the jail. Who could judge so smugly? You just have to try and steer a steady ship, and hope. Bail out if you have to. Hold on. Love them in all their complexity. Forgive.

There are parents who witter endlessly about their successful children; their own standing in life fiercely twinned to their offsprings' achievements. Yet the mortifying, embarrassing falls are rarely talked about because we feel they reflect on us as parents too. But we all have our battles to face. A reader, Glen, wrote, 'For me, still in the thick of parenthood, having four kids you can talk about feels more like luck than anything else.' Oh yes. All of us trying to work it out, hoping everything will be fine, patching up the dam. But it may burst one day. With any of us.

*

260

Laugh with the kids more, nag a little less. I remind myself of this often now, with the on-the-cusp, almost-men in my midst. Who we're about to lose as they stride into their own lives. We revel in them, just that. So much more so after their Nonna's death. Looking to the living, loving them, holding on. Just that.

*

The lanterns are complete. Nothing like the smooth originals. A pale map of a journey with river lines of gold threaded through them. They cup a tea light candle just as they used to; are once again our little cylinders of stilling light. But they shine a different beauty now. Patched up, scarred, endearing, in their very human scale. They embody a careful, grateful love.

*

Slowly, slowly, I am – we are – being put back together. By life. The sheer insistence of it. Whole, differently whole. As Colette said, 'No one asked you to be happy. Get to work.' So I do. It's been too long. Elayn, after all, taught strength.

*

Would Elayn have considered her death faithful to the original meaning of euthanasia – the 'good death'? I'm sure, in her mind, yes. In hindsight though, if she had been granted the gift of after-thought, I wonder.

I think she had little consideration for all of those who had to deal with the aftermath.

*

'Look at how Elayn chose to die,' comments a friend who knew us both. 'She shut herself off. Did it alone. Removed herself. As she had done so many times in her life.' The booze and the drugs on that final day. Was it an enormous, furious, fit of pique? Let it go, let it go. We will never know.

*

If you were faced with what Elayn was faced with, would you do things differently? I would do it Helena's way. With dialogue. Thoughtfulness. Instruction. I would not hold my family hostage by secrecy and withholding, would not inflict such a cataclysmic shock upon them. I don't think Elayn had any idea of the catastrophe she unleashed upon so many lives.

*

Imperfection is the egg stain on the poet's hand-knitted jumper. The hole that resembles a bullet's trajectory in the back of the moth-eaten tweed jacket. The watery ring-mark left on the antique wooden table. The crack in a ceramic lantern. The flawed but often loving mother. All the imperfections that are maps of living. Living well, living deeply, living.

*

A Japanese legend. A young man, Sen no Rikyu, wanted to learn the elaborate ritual that is The Way of Tea. He visited a great tea-master, Takeno Joo. Asked permission to tend Joo's garden. Rikyu cleaned and tidied and raked, then clean and tidied and raked again. He stepped back. Examined the result. Noted the perfection. Then just before showing it to the great master, Rikyu grabbed a cherry tree's trunk and shook it. A few flowers spilled to the ground. The look of the entire scene was transformed. In that one swift movement Rikyu had introduced disorder and mess. By doing so, he had introduced humanity. Life.

Rikyu is revered in Japan as one who understood to his core the concept of *wabi-sabi*. The art of finding beauty in imperfection. Profundity in earthiness. The art of honouring authenticity above all. Everything that today's technology-saturated culture isn't. *Wabi-sabi* is the jumbly energy of flea markets as opposed to shopping centres, a spiky protea as opposed to a dozen unscented roses. *Wabi-sabi* celebrates cracks and crevices, ruts and rot, a softening by time and the knocks of life. It embraces both the glory and melancholy of a life well lived; the complexity. Its ceramic embodiment is *Kintsugi*.

*

With jagged edges and sharp textures the shattered ceramic lanterns take their place among their more perfect cousins. Startling in their new beauty. The joins are visible and there are gaps where chips have disappeared and some of the lanterns no longer sit flush on a surface; they are what they were, with visible fault lines. My favourites now, because they have a very human narrative attached to them. They are complete.

25

Do I support euthanasia?

At the fraught beginning of this journey, no. I was drowning in moral uncertainty, shock, anger. At all of it, the entire movement, for whisking my mother from me; too easily and too silently. It had stolen her from us. But now, a softening. Because of the lonely journey Elayn ultimately embarked upon. It shouldn't have been like that. If we do not reconsider our euthanasia laws we are condemning the person who wants to die to a hideously bleak and lonely death. For if they carefully research the legal and emotional situation, as Elayn did, they will come to the conclusion that the least messy way to enact death is to go it alone. To protect their family. There has to be a better way. Governments have to enable it, or there will be too many future Elayns.

*

The embracing of individual choice is the mark of a mature nation. As we advance as a society there's an inevitability to the embracing of euthanasia; as we become more empowered as individuals, more insistent. As we turn away from our organised religions with their thundering voices and dubious moral authority in the face of human suffering. As we consider a future of a rapidly aging population, with increased instances of chronic pain, and drugs that do not work well enough.

Elayn had to go underground. Her family never had the chance to have the rational conversation with her about what she really wanted to do. If pro-euthanasia laws had been in place this entire situation would have been far less messy. We need the laws out of compassion for people wanting to die, and out of compassion for their loved ones. It's too hard, too messy, the other way. If the right to a dignified death had been legal none of this would have been a problem for Elayn. Or for us. Her death would still have been painful, but the aftermath would not have been one of such traumatic entanglement.

*

Consider the ethical philosophy that goes all the way back to the *Meno*, a Socratic dialogue written by Plato. That the reasonable man – the sentient person – has a right to self-determination, which by self-evident corollary, includes a right to die. With wisdom and humanity. As the Western world veers into unstoppable rationality.

*

Among our elderly, chronic pain seems like a stigmatised world of silence and suffering where not enough information about alternative methods of pain control is getting through. Doctors need to embrace change, as do governments. The right to die, legally, feels like an unstoppable need that will be embraced by all jurisdictions in the Western world eventually. That will bring openness, discussion. An enabling supported by the medical profession. And most importantly, family. Because we need to listen. To step into the shoes of the chronic pain sufferer, and understand.

*

Would I vote for euthanasia if ever there was a referendum on it? Yes. Because I'm in favour of the freedom to choose. And Helena's way is the best way, and none of us should be denied that choice. If Elayn had had the means to do what Helena has planned so carefully then my family would have had the solace of knowledge. We could have faced the journey together, with preparation and calmness, with celebration and care. My mother went underground. Did it her way, with a despairing loneliness, because it is not a legal right to end your life, with dignity, in this country.

Elayn has taught me and changed me. Such a fierce seizer of life would not have gone quietly into death unless she was at the bleak, irreversible end of her tether. A raging will to live blazes in most of us. And most will not abuse that gift of choice.

As Philip Nitschke says, 'Elayn was reflective of a very deep-seated human desire for individual autonomy; as a highly motivated woman she was clear about what she did not want. None of us would ever elect death over life if we could help it. But there comes a time when acceptance that we will die is complete, and the next stage is about easing that process to the best of our abilities. Far from taking a "coward's" route, those who seek to exact control over the dying process are pragmatic and directed, and in knowing the end result, taking that step is nothing short of courageous; the bitter-sweet end of a life and an immediate end of present pain.'

*

Mum, I suspect, spent much of her final days curled up in agony, in the foetal position, just wanting the pain to go away. She was frightened. Alone. Heavily dosed up on her drugs. Her bleak last days feel like they were marked by despair and anguish; overwhelmed by hopelessness. She felt that there was no way out of this.

If she had had the peace of mind of a Dignitas, here in Australia, she would have lived her final years to the fullest knowing that she had the comfort of a dignified exit ahead of her, at the time of her choosing. She would have passed away surrounded by love. That knowledge would have released her, in her final years of life, to seize the joy.

As Helena has so carefully planned to do. She has spent her last year on earth revelling in family and mates and concerts and travel and champagne high teas and celebratory tattoos and five star hotels. Everything Elayn would have loved; everything she would normally be diving right in to (except, perhaps, the tattoos; but you never know). Helena wants her last hours to be spent in a room brimming with love, with just her immediate family and her best friend and herself. And in her last minutes they will all be holding hands, until she slips away. Mum never had that anchor of solace in her final years, never had the security of knowing there was a potential release from the anguish. All she had was the pain and the weight of the secrecy. The despair.

And a Dignitas in Australia might have prevented her from going so soon, as its rigorous checks and balances would most likely have sent warning signals to the medical assessors that Elayn had not thoroughly investigated all avenues of pain relief; that there were alternatives out there. A Dignitas could have saved her, for all of us who loved her so much, for a little longer; saved her from the bleakness of her lonely death. A Dignitas would have given her much needed peace of mind.

Living new. Beyond flung words and felling silences Elayn's courage was a gift. The family can't control losing her, there was no choice in that. The choice now is: what are we going to do with this? How can we somehow glean the positive from it? The end is the start.

*

As a family we talk about Nonna a lot. Pray before children's bedtimes for her, have an increased number of photos around the house. Ticky has six blu-tacked in a shrine above his desk. If her favourite songs or movies come into our lives we tip a hat. Speak of her, reminisce, keep her alive in our hearts. And by this. These words. It is her turn now. What Elayn always wanted, what we all want. The gift of attention.

*

Katherine Mansfield of her mother, in her journals: 'She lived every moment of life more fully and completely than anyone I've ever known – and her gaiety wasn't any less real for being high courage – courage to meet anything with.' Elayn demonstrated high courage repeatedly with her audacious choices. From her teens onwards she was

271

restless with the path laid out for her by others. She needed transformation, escape, and acted on it. From the desert of her childhood. The country town of her teenage years. The suburban trap of her married world. And eventually, finally, from life.

Gratitude, now, for the high courage Elayn taught both my daughter and myself. 'You cannot find peace by avoiding life,' Virginia Woolf wrote. And so I dive back into it because it can be avoided no longer. Have to find peace within it, not removed from it.

*

Elayn wore her nudity like an armour of modernity. I never wanted her style, her loucheness, her topless swims; her diet belt that whirred around her waist from a central pole in front of her that was meant to, somehow, wobble off the fat; her ridiculous high-heeled shoes that robbed her of comfort. She hated my daughterly judgment. To me, she was surface. She felt the chill of my judgment as I felt the chill of hers. How ridiculous it all seems now.

*

The gulf between us roared back into our relationship on the final night I saw Elayn. She wanted me to do an illegal U-turn across double lines into incoming traffic to get

272

her cash out, on the other side of the road. I snapped that no, I'd do it my way. Which meant driving two hundred metres down the road and turning left into a side street then doing a legal U-turn and turning back onto the main road, at traffic lights. We both flinched into an old, wounded silence. Still capable of the ancient ways, the familiar ruts of hurt. Then Elayn withdrew her money and I drove her on to the enveloping of family, my family, who she loved so much. But all through that final birthday dinner was the memory of the injured silence, over both of us. As I drove Elayn back to her flat I put it aside and told Mum that I wanted to check in with her every day from now on. She said all right. Commented on what a happy, close community I had around me. How strong it was, how lucky Andrew and I were. I agreed. We were both learning to move on.

*

Yet we had come full circle as mother and child. Found our way back into acceptance, and love. It was a step into maturity.

And so I climb out of the lair, hold a face to the light. No longer so violently twinned to this situation. I feel an immense unlocking. A miraculous calm after the furious raging of a storm that has been at the centre of my life, for my entire life. It's gone. Extinguished.

273

I have been rescued. By this. Writing. To understand. It has hauled me out. The prospect: a renovation of serenity. And so I begin again by doing what I really want to do. Work. Aspiring to an existence with a lot of quiet in it. Turning from people I don't need in my life. Shunning bitsy busyness. Finding the courage to say no. I need to be good at being alive again.

*

My body has been locked in its own battle with stress. But then quite suddenly it clears. Months down the track I realise I'm righted. The loosening has happened quietly of its own accord. A lightness has come back, just like that.

Striding into the light.

*

Elayn was an iceberg, with the bright blast of her above the surface then the great, murky mass that we knew little of underneath the water. Vivaciously public yet secretive; barely speaking to friends about the euthanasia time bomb at the centre of her later life. She put on a damned good show.

*

'Energy is eternal delight,' William Blake said. And that was Elayn. What will never be forgotten: the beguiling lift of her energy. Energy is seductive. Energy is enthusiasm. Energy is life.

*

The good times. Holding on to them. The relief, in a visit after my daughter was born, of Elayn being fine. A new female in the family had broken the intensity; soldered us. How miraculous that a little girl in our midst would unite us. As if there had been something unsavoury about how we'd been for so long, as if Elayn and I had to grow up. To shield this fresh new female life from it.

*

My eight-year-old daughter laughs at me now as I do Zumba; not cruelly, but still, she's laughing. Just as I used to at Elayn, yet the dancing I'm doing now is the dancing of my mother, just as Biahbi's dancing will one day be mine but she doesn't know this yet. I hope I never disappoint her as much as I disappointed my mother. But it's out of my hands. I was never enraptured by Elayn, just as my daughter is not enraptured by me. I had a difficult relationship with my mother, as she did with her mother, yet I'm determined not to repeat the pattern. I know that the relationship between mothers and daughters can often be fragile, a landscape prickly with hurt and shock. But I will do everything in my power to never push my daughter away.

For fathers and daughters, it's often different. Andrew and Biahbi have a fervent, forgiving bond that feels unassailable, shutting me out. I'm okay with that; I have it with Bob too. The difference between Elayn and me: I celebrate it. Am grateful for it. There is no competitiveness.

*

Suffering should always open the door to wisdom.

26

Six months since the writing was begun, the maelstrom of bewilderment that was this book. Now, finally, stilled. The blanket is drawn up, I am tunnelled in warmth. Writing is, has always been, a response to a deep perplexity. An excavation of the truth.

Writing is a response to a wound of the heart. And a pen is a furious balm.

*

V, the counsellor, tells me there could have been a million reasons why Elayn did what she did, and it's extremely common to feel guilt in these situations.

She tells me my mother was terribly conflicted. At the end of her life she did something out of love – a birthday dinner. Then something out of anger – a suicide. 'I think the reasons were in her, not you.' V adds, 'Elayn was angry all her life.' My mother waged an almighty battle before death, with herself, that no one was privy to. It was a complex death. She is the anchor to a world of pain, pinning me down, and I have to cast myself adrift to survive. And kick towards the light.

*

What has been learnt: that the greatest chasm between two people – out of all the chasms that can swamp – is love withheld, by a parent. If you want to do the most damage, try messing with that most primal of human bonds. Love withheld, as a weapon, can lock up a life. Elayn's love was like black market money – there was nowhere secure to deposit it. I could never hold onto it strongly enough. The love would overwhelm with its bounteousness then be flintily withdrawn. For desert-months.

*

Love is all you need from a parent. Like milk. The sun. A blanket on a cold night. Ben Okri wrote that we should learn to extricate ourselves from all the things that have moulded us, which possibly limit our free and undiscovered road. I had to free myself from a parent who knew nothing of my secret road. Yet does any parent, of any child?

*

With Elayn I acted volcanically. It was pure, ugly emotion; a heart pumping with love. Outrage. Pique. I never grew up with the expectation that my mother would wrap me in her arms and love me unconditionally; would look after me. The solitude of love. She is more arrestingly with me dead than alive, her absence a presence.

Marguerite Duras said, 'our mothers always remain the strangest, craziest people we've ever met,' and this feels true, perhaps because mothers can show their daughters their raw, ugly, complicated selves like no one else does.

I am still recognising wounds from childhood for what they are now, back from when my parents' marriage fractured. In middle age, several years ago, I had been feeling suddenly, inexplicably, raw; deeply vulnerable and grieving about my parents' breakup when I was ten, about my father's remarriage and my imploded nuclear family.

What was this unbearable fresh hurt within me? But then came the accepting. That no one is perfect, least of all myself, and that everyone you come across is your teacher in some way. How are you growing from the experience of knowing them? And with that came a release into joy like sparks flying off an anvil.

*

For much of my adult existence. I wanted to live a big life – just not Elayn's big life. I never wanted to be a woman where fear dictated every choice. She didn't either. She was a good teacher.

*

One day, in the thick of the warfare yet again, I recalled Lexi's words about the woman who did a good deed every day of her life and lived by that creed. I rang Mum after a period of non-speaking. The relief of the love on the end of the phone. The glow of everything being all right. We both wanted this. But only one of us took the next step, always took the next step.

*

Laved. How I love that word and long for the salve of it. It means pouring water upon, washing, soothing. Laved, and lumen. Good, strong, lit words. 'I beseech you enter your life,' Ezra Pound wrote. Yes, it is time.

*

Once, in my mid-forties, I made a trip to Sydney from London. Elayn and I were good. I did not ask her if I could stay with her, I'd learnt. I checked into the Hilton and she visited. She liked this. I wasn't intruding into her world. I wondered on that trip if she was vicious to me, during all those years of exile, because I'd chosen to leave her? Because hurting someone is sometimes the only way of holding them. And was there something of that in her final act? A plea to be noticed. To be etched like acid into all our lives.

*

On the top shelf of Boh's bookcase, the carcass of a yellow balloon. Stabbed in anger at Nonna's funeral. He kept it in the pocket of his school shorts. And now it's a memorial to his beloved, complex grandmother. Next to a collector's Batman car and a strip of party photos from a photo booth. The things we keep. All the children, hurtling into a growing up.

*

This is a story of now, about old people slipping through the cracks in the cram of life's whoosh. About dignity. Choice. A clash of generations. Guilt. About slipping away because you don't want to be a bother to anyone – but by doing so you become more of a bother to everyone close than you've ever been in your life. It was all quite magnificently her. So, very, Elayn.

*

'For we think back through our mothers if we are women,' Virginia Woolf wrote. No one shapes our lives more, as girls and as women, than them. Katherine Mansfield said the mind she loved must have wild places in it. My mother's mind did and I loved her for those wild places that blazed freedom and spontaneity and vivaciousness and courage and reclusiveness; a love of the mysterious, replenishing alone. She loved to ring-fence her solitude, as do I.

*

What is lost: the complexity of Elayn. She wasn't evil, or bad, or wicked. She was just a woman. A contradictory, wounded, thinking, empowered, impetuous, exhausted, mighty woman. She chose, most often, a fighter's path. No female has had a stronger presence. It was never indifferent. Even her silences were volatile. Strike a match to them and boomph, immolation. Everything was vivid. The love of my life, and the hate of my life.

*

'Grief is the price we pay for love,' Queen Elizabeth said in her message to the United States after the 9/11 attacks. With Elayn there is grief; tremendous, demolishing grief; and because of that, of course, so must there be love. Tremendous. Demolishing.

*

Elayn created disturbance. As books should, as women should.

*

Men got in the way of my mother. They complicated her world. She had lived heroically for so long. She was always trying to end complication, and her final act was a way to end complication. She wanted the medicine of simplicity. Don't we all?

*

Elayn never reduced herself, as a woman, as a wife; never allowed herself to be rubbed out. She refused to be trapped in a proscribed life. Her lesson: don't succumb.

*

I've never been a perfume person but now I am wearing Elayn's White Linen. Slipping into her way of being; wanting my children to have a particular 'mother scent'; stamping the memory of me, and her, into them.

*

Anthony Burgess said that literature thrives on taboos. This is taboo:

- I wished my mother dead at times. Wished for the relief of that, the release. How wrong I was. There was no release in her death. Only a tightening of the grip.
- Elayn was at once at the centre and the periphery of my little family. We were all so busy. She stamped my life more strikingly than any other person yet I should have allowed her more space in it, as she should have with me. Two wary women, circling each other.
- There was a visceral horror of her closing over me. She tried to form me yet I spent my entire life trying to unform that image she had of me. My mother, my home-born enemy.

*

Our eldest brother was less savaged by Elayn than either Paul or myself so he is not a part of this story. Indeed, he would have a different story. He is on a different path, in a different life. No sibling can speak for another.

*

Elayn was careful never to disclose her age. I honoured that at her funeral, and in this book.

*

Lu Frank, a reader, wrote of her mother: 'I had dreadful guilts up until this year over so many missed opportunities. We were like chalk and cheese, and if we had one wonderful day the next would be terrible and I'd spend it broken hearted. But I heard someone saying: "You can rewrite your story … by forgiving yourself. Saying over and over the good times. If I had more experience I would do it differently. The past is finished. Move on. Remember the best bits." I now feel much, much better, having resolved and changed my slant on things.'

Every day back then was a tricky and tenuous experiment. But every day now, I remember the bravery, the audacity, the smile, the dazzle. Selective remembering. For survival.

*

A great giggly smile coming over my hours. I am back. Elayn will never quite hold me. Because she conveyed the impression that children did not complete her but reduced her. She made me feel a colossal loneliness within my blood family; that I wasn't quite right.

Now, I have a determination to mother differently. The tea lights glow in their lanterns. Something has recalibrated. 'You feel the bands break that were riveted about your heart,' Gertrude Bell wrote and yes, yes. Sleeping with the abandonment of a child again, limbs splayed. The world a vast yes again, freshly yes.

*

It feels like a rifle butt has been jammed into my heart for so long and now, finally, it's removed.

So I turn inward to what's always been there – family. Not the family I've held restlessly in my blood all my life but the family created around me. So it is Andrew. Ticky, Boh, Biahbi, Jages. They rescue me and don't even know it. The gratitude for them, and it's never said enough. My sanctuary, my harbour, my rest from the toss of the world. Here, at home, in this place. I will stop running, make a go of this.

My world flying open again, like a door into light.

*

I marvel at friends who have a closeness with their mothers like a deep, best friendship. My daughter loves me with a physicality almost sexual – tenderly kisses me, pulls me to her, demands the fiercest of cuddles; her want draining mine as she drapes herself over me and slips her limbs into mine.

I do not stop it or push it away because I've endured a lifetime of a mother withholding. And this is a tonic. Firming me for the world.

*

Remembering the blazing moments: sleeping in a tight bed with Elayn in Japan; going to three movies in a row in one of our marathon sessions, crying with her for five minutes after watching *Breaking the Waves*; gulping individual chocolates from the trays of boutique chocolate shops together; marvelling over the Winged Victory of Samothrace in Paris and the unicorn tapestries in New York and a bowl with river lines of *Kintsugi* in Tokyo; yakking and yarning about neighbours, shopkeepers and superstars; because we could bare our truly ugly, gossipy underbellies to each other and no one else, and get it. And I know that everything was all right, really. We had love. It was okay. And I am as flawed as she was.

*

Most of all, just missing her. Even though she had held my life hostage for so much of it. She always filled it up, even by absence. The disbelief that she is not here now. The rangy absence of her. Every day the absence.

*

Why are daughters so incurious about their own mothers' lives? What sin was committed here? I never had an inkling about why my parents split up, never questioned it deeply. And now I am on the wrong side of Elayn's narrative. An outsider to her story. I chose not to access it while I could; never made much of an effort to be on the right side. That flinty acceleration of the next generation into a new era, new lives. And then suddenly, of course, it's too late.

*

V's definition of a mother: someone who provides shelter. Comfort. Support. Had my mother provided any of these? Not as an adult. We did not have black murderous rages in our family, we had silences. The piracy of silence. And now it is gone. It is good. There is a lot of good.

*

In some of the beautiful old art deco cinemas still dotted forlornly around Australia, there used to be what is known as the crying room.

It was a room reserved for mothers, where they could place their babies in a line of cots while they watched a film and got a break. But if the baby cried the number of the cot would flash on the screen and the mother would come back and tend to her child. Some of the crying rooms had glass inserts in the wall so the film could still be watched.

I imagine an Elayn dreaming her whole life of that crying room; a place to deposit her children while she grabbed at life, gulped the world; I imagine her walking away from the cinema and never coming back. But she did, always did. As I said earlier, whenever I was sick she'd hold me and hold me as if she wanted to leech the illness from me; in some elemental maternal embrace involving a sick child and their mother. We all have untidy lives.

*

It's a universal desire to be needed. Elayn gave me the gift of being needed at the end of her life. A week before her death I picked her up from a scanning centre and drove her home. She was teary with pain as I helped her into the car. 'It's so good to be with you, Nik. You're so calming.' I hold on to that. This world is seamed rich. Layers and layers of wonder. Yet in the end Elayn saw it as full of nothing. That's what pain did to her. She just wanted it stopped.

*

I see it now: if Elayn had emailed me a more specific note on her final night, a note of farewell and fulsome love, I would have rushed around and stopped her doing whatever she was about to do. Suddenly my mind flies open, like a door into dazzling day.

As I age my heart is growing young. Because the anger over my mother, anger that has fuelled and swamped and blighted my entire life, is now snuffed. That is something to celebrate.

*

The way of Kabbalah: tragedy cracks you open so your light can shine. And at some point you have to make the decision to open your life to the necessary warmth, to start living again; like a plant turning to the sun, spining yourself tall within the light. A decision you have to make.

*

Helena, dear, brave, Helena: she said to me, one day: "'You can be me when I'm gone" is a classic line from one of Neil Gaiman's Sandman books. My youngest son and I strongly identify with it. The whole concept is that the man goes, dies – and leaves his son to be him when he goes. That's us in a nutshell. And it's why I'm so concerned about him because I know he's going to take me with him when I go. And I know that even though intellectually and emotionally he's as prepared as anyone can be (about euthanasia of a parent), it's going to hit him harder than what he thinks it's going to.'

My heart goes out to that beautiful boy in his early twenties. He thinks he can prepare for the considered death of his mother adequately, carefully, slowly, but he cannot.

*

Helena has chosen the best way to die by your own hand, given her circumstances. By dying she is releasing her children to who they should be. She is enabling them to complete their growing up, and this cannot happen while she is with them. They will become someone else after she is gone. It is progression.

*

The intention: to live differently. Parent differently. To live honestly with my children; communicate strongly and clearly with them. To never spring a death by my own hand upon them, to never leave them so skinned.

*

Our little diminishing family cannot be broken. As no family can. There is something too fundamental there. Too much memory, history. Our family is threaded through with a resin of gold now and it is strong. We have come through this. More tender now; with each other, with the outside world. Our edges softened by sorrow.

*

A spontaneous road trip with Biahbi. Sometimes we just have to flee the boy energy (times four) in our house and they let us – grateful to be temporarily rid of us, mad things that we are.

We're singing songs in the car, loudly, joyously, like no one's watching, but Biahbi breaks off to tell me I'm really, really not cool. 'You never were, Mum.' Ah, the wisdom of the eight year old, and we haven't even hit fifteen yet. I laugh with her.

I'll be treading carefully with this one. She's singular and sparky and strong, with a loud, uncrushable voice. Elayn has taught me how to be with her. I will love her differently, as a daughter; I do love her differently. With celebration and affirmation and chuff. With understanding that we are differently complex females. And with a knowledge that we have to go easy on each other.

Like Win, like Elayn, we both prize control. We kick out strongly against a shaping of us.

I hold my hand out the car window and butt the breeze on the highway. Biahbi laughs and does the same. We grin, each to each. A mother and daughter, twinned strong. I am freshly carefree, differently able. Something has been cauterised.

*

To hold on to: Elayn's magnificence, most of all. And the understanding, and forgiveness, of the multitudes that we all carry within us.

*

The grief is not over, it never will be over. It still trips me up in unexpected moments, stumbling me all over again. What does it: a reminisce with Paul, the sight of a mate laughing so easily with their mum, a Klimt painting we both loved. Simple things. Two steps forward, one step back, righting myself and then not.

But the moving forward is stronger, swifter now; the seam of melancholy more hidden. Yes, climbing back into the world, firm.

*

I feel I am fully a woman now. Stronger, wiser. Little binding scars all over my life but laughing again and it's like a hat flying off into the sun. The sheer, glorious whoop of it. This rescue, finally, shines.

293

*

In the Grand Ballroom of Destiny Reversal Elayn has once again triumphed. I hold the joyous memory of her, and everything she did for me, in the fist of my heart.

When anything interesting happens I want to tell her. I want to tell her this. All this.

PICTURES

ACKNOWLEDGEMENTS

A tough journey made buoyant by the good women of HarperCollins: Mary Rennie for saying there was a book in this complex situation in the first place. Catherine Milne for her fierce intelligence. Nicola Robinson for her compassionate sincerity. Jaki Arthur for being one of the best in her business. And Shona Martyn, dear Shona, for her enthusiasm and passion, squeals and squeaks; and for the depth of the wisdom most of all. Thank you, madam, for fourteen fabulous years of publishing. I cannot imagine the writerly path without you by my side, but walk along it I now must. You will be terribly missed.

To James Kellow: for nurturing this extraordinary team.

To my editors at *The Australian*, Christine Middap and Michelle Gunn: for teaching me so much.

To my agents David Godwin and Kirsty McLachlan: for twenty years of thoughtful guidance. I wish we were geographically closer.

To Philip Nitschke: it could have been adversorial; it was unexpectedly nourishing.

To all my girlfriends: for the flowers, the laughs, the spag bols and the necessary texts when needed. Thank you for checking in.

To Helena, darling Helena: for the joy and the wisdom, the grace and generosity, which will guide me through the rest of my days. Thank you for teaching me how to live.

To Paul, Bob and the Oodies, for seeing me through this; and to the Chap, the dear, beleaguered Chap, who's had to put up with so much. My heart is brimmed with love for you all. Thank you for saving me, again and again, and keeping me laughing.

And to Elayn, for making me who I am.

ELAINE GEMMELL
HEIGHT: 5 ft. 3 ins.
BUST: 32 ins. WAIST: 22 ins. HIPS: 32 ins.
HAIR: Brunette. EYES: Hazel.
Photographic Model, Mannequin, TV.